Stephen Drether MD

Lloyd Axelrod MD

Willard Daggett, MD

Voices

of the

Massachusetts General Hospital

1950–2000

Wit, Wisdom and Untold Tales

Chair: Stephen P. Dretler, MD
Editor: Lloyd Axelrod, MD
Co-Editors: Willard M. Daggett, MD
Georgia W. Peirce

Lamprey & Lee
an imprint of Bibliomotion, Inc.

First published in 2014 by Lamprey & Lee,
an imprint of Bibliomotion, Inc.

39 Harvard Street
Brookline, MA 02445

Tel: 617.934.2427
www.bibliomotion.com

Printed in the United States of America

Library of Congress Cataloging-in-Publication Data

Voices of the Massachusetts General Hospital 1950-2000: wit, wisdom and untold tales / chair,
Stephen P. Dretler; editor, Lloyd Axelrod; co-editors: Willard M. Daggett, Georgia W. Peirce.
    p. ; cm.
  Includes index.
  ISBN 978-1-942108-02-3 (hardcover : alk. paper) – ISBN 978-1-942108-03-0 (ebook)
  I. Dretler, Stephen P., 1938-, editor. II. Axelrod, Lloyd, editor. III. Daggett, Willard M., editor. IV.
Peirce, Georgia W., editor.
  [DNLM: 1. Massachusetts General Hospital. 2. Hospitals, General–Boston–Anecdotes. 3.
Hospitals, General–Boston–Humor. 4. Hospitals, General–Boston–Personal Narratives. 5.
History, 20th Century–Boston. 6. Hospitals, General–history–Boston. WX 28 AM4]
  RA982.B7
  362.1109744'61–dc23
                                                                    2014041153

TABLE OF CONTENTS

ACKNOWLEDGMENTS

We are indebted to ever so many people who willingly and enthusiastically assisted in the preparation of this book.

This publication would not have been possible without the help of the hundreds of people who responded to our request for aphorisms, sayings, anecdotes, stories and tales, only some of which we were able to include in this volume. We also appreciate the efforts of the many colleagues and friends who provided the biographical notes and stories that give this book its unique character.

Jeff Mifflin, archivist of the MGH, and Christine Moynihan, intern of the MGH Archives and Special Collections, provided valuable images and documents. Paul Batista, senior medical photographer, MGH Photography Department, graciously obliged our many requests for photographs, old and new. Arch MacInnes, director of publications for the MGH Public Affairs Office, was our indispensable designer and adviser in preparing our manuscript for publication. Sarah Alger, the director of the Paul S. Russell, MD Museum of Medical History and Innovation, provided valuable help and advice in the process of publication. Paul S. Russell, MD, and Jeanette Ives Erickson, RN, DNP, provided valuable encouragement, advice and support from the beginning of the project until its end.

This project began in response to a request from the Russell Museum for a display of meaningful and memorable quotations from MGH physicians and nurses and evolved into this volume. We welcomed the challenge to fulfill this request and thank the leaders of the museum for the opportunity to work together on this project.

So much of what we do at the MGH, and so much of the content of this book, involves teaching and learning. We wish to acknowledge our many teachers at the MGH and the MGH School of Nursing for their profound wisdom, consistent brilliance, timely wit, genuine compassion and enduring commitment. The inclusion of many who are deceased brought them to life again for us, and we hope for you.

It is especially meaningful to us that the preparation of this volume provided us with the opportunity to interact with such a large, diverse, gracious and creative group of people.

INTRODUCTION

Voices of the Massachusetts General Hospital 1950–2000 is a compilation of wise sayings, sober advice, clever aphorisms, purposeful humor, meaningful wit and touching anecdotes. This collection was assembled in response to e-mail requests sent to approximately 3,000 residents and staff physicians and hundreds of nurses who trained or practiced at the MGH between 1950 and 2000. Department archives were mined for electronic lists of physicians and nurses and requests were made for recollections of memorable and meaningful quotes or stories. Approximately 250 responses were returned. These were evaluated for their relevance to clinical care, teaching, research and a fourth category entitled MGH Values. The latter are principles of patient care that may be found at many institutions but at the MGH constitute a code of which we are proud and by which we are committed to live.

You may note that not every distinguished MGH physician or nurse who served between 1950 and 2000 is included. This is a consequence of the way we solicited contributions. This volume is not a systematic history of the MGH during this period. It is a compilation from the hearts and minds of those who responded to our request. We are aware that most of the physicians are white men and most of the nurses are white women, reflecting the reality of our institution and the society in which it functioned during this time interval. We are confident that if this exercise were to be repeated for 2001–2050, or even for the last decade, one would find a rich diversity of personnel reflecting our inclusive values and the changed reality of the world from which our staff is drawn.

Additionally, we have included bits of otherwise unavailable and previously unreported MGH lore and a few stories of MGH traditions that are only known by those of us who have had the privilege of spending our professional lives within these walls.

It is our hope that you will be moved and enriched by our colleagues' compassion and wisdom.

THE DOCTORS

THE NURSES

Eleanor Roosevelt, child with polio and Walter Bauer, MD

PATIENT CARE

■ Paul Dudley White, MD

"There are three important principles in the treatment of disease. Prevention. Prevention. Prevention."

"Listen to what the *patient* can tell you – it may be more important than anything else you do."

"I am realizing that to get the most out of clinical cases one must see and help in considerable experimental work where fundamental principles are brought out and worked upon. My ideas have quite undergone a revolution in this respect – I've always paid more attention to results without first having grounded myself in elements."

— from a letter to his mother written on December 21, 1913, while studying in London

Dr. White with his patient, President Dwight D. Eisenhower

Born in Roxbury, Massachusetts, Dr. Paul Dudley White came to the MGH from Harvard Medical School as an intern in 1911. Originally interested in pediatrics, he turned his attention to cardiology after spending a year in London working with the famous cardiac physiologist Sir Thomas Lewis. He returned to the MGH to found the Cardiac Unit in 1916 – the first such subspecialty clinic dedicated to the treatment of heart disease in the United States. He served with the MGH Base Hospital No. 6 in World War I, after which he returned to the MGH to pursue has illustrious career.

Over the next several years, he achieved an international reputation as one of the leading cardiologists – if not THE leading cardiologist – of his time. His reputation was further enhanced when he was asked to serve as the cardiologist to President Dwight D. Eisenhower after the president had a heart attack in 1955. Dr. White resigned as chief of the MGH Cardiac Unit in 1948 to chair the committee that established the National Heart Institute. He was one of the founders of the American Heart Association.

A man of boundless energy, he was one of the first physicians to educate the public on the importance of exercise, not smoking and a prudent diet in the prevention of heart disease. He was professionally active until the time of his death in 1973 at the age of 87.

Biographical note prepared by Roman W. DeSanctis, MD

■ Walter Bauer, MD

**Walter Bauer emphasized that admitting that
one does not know reflects integrity and is
essential to caring for patients.
He further felt that acknowledging ignorance
is the first step in substituting knowledge for dogma.**

— *submitted by K. Frank Austen, MD*

**"This hospital has three goals –
1. to take care of patients;
2. to teach the next generation; and
3. to do research.
Don't you ever forget which comes first."**

I came to the MGH as an intern in July 1951; Walter Bauer was the just appointed chief of Medicine. He was a highly successful academic clinician, had a strong personality, was a leader of young doctors and had extraordinary vision for the organization of his new department.

In 1961 he appointed me chief of the Arthritis Unit but glossed over the fact that I had no training in the discipline. He set me up with a laboratory, helped me obtain grants to fund it and provided me with reluctant trainees. A good example was Robert Pinals, who had been at Tufts, was recently discharged from the Army and expected to be working with Evan Calkins, whom Dr. Bauer appointed to succeed him as chief of the Arthritis Group. Evan did a fine job but after a few years was offered the position of chief of Medicine and professor at the University of Buffalo Medical School, and he couldn't resist. Evan was a few years older than I, but I sort of ranked with him as a fellow former chief medical resident.

Pinals wasn't impressed; he marched into the Bauer office to complain. Bauer inhaled on one of his many cigarettes that day, exhaled and told Bob, "That's OK, Pinals, you and Krane can learn about arthritis (it wasn't 'rheumatology' then) together." Bob slumped out of the room, but he eventually cheered up and we did learn together, and remain friends. Unfortunately, the chief succumbed to severe chronic pulmonary disease two years later. I still miss him.

Biographical note prepared by Stephen M. Krane, MD

Edwin H. Cassem, SJ, MD

"When caring for a severely debilitated or dying patient, always treat him and address him as you would if he were still on top of his game."

— on showing proper respect for severely debilitated patients

One day Ned was called by the nurses to a surgical floor because of a patient whose behavior was so obnoxious that none wanted to care for her, and all were afraid even to enter her room. After a while the nurses were surprised to hear Ned's familiar bellowing laughter ringing from her bedside. A half hour later Ned emerged from her room with a broad, impish smile. They implored Ned to tell all. He did. In his conversation with her, a diabetic, a double above-the-knee amputee, he had learned that in her younger years she had been a track star and a celebrated national champion women's high hurdler, and had competed for her country in the 1960 Olympics in Rome. His story was a "game changer" for both the nurses and the more clearly for the legless runner they could now care for.

Ned Cassem grew up in Omaha, Nebraska and came east. His fierce religious devotion was harnessed to a prodigious intellect, powering a career legendary for its impact on medicine, psychiatry and, particularly, medical caring at the end of life. For generations of devoted students and patients, Ned was an exemplar of the Jesuit principle of "spirituality for decision makers." He pioneered the MGH Optimum Care Committee, a safe forum for clinicians, ethicists and legal counsel to engage in shared debate and deliberation over some of MGH's most profound clinical challenges.

After Tom Hackett's untimely death in 1988, Ned, always derisive of "administration," dutifully took the reins and led the department unflinchingly through a challenging decade with his characteristic balance of uncompromising adherence to truth and uncommon gentleness.

Biographical note prepared by John B. Herman, MD

Roman W. DeSanctis, MD

**"Whatever external forces conspire to
make the medical practice more frustrating and
difficult, the essence of medicine remains the
encounter between the doctor and the patient."**

**"I am so privileged to be a physician;
I go to work every day with no other mandate
than to relieve pain and suffering and to heal the sick.
What a noble calling this is."**

*— from Roman's acceptance speech at the awarding
of the MGPO Trustees Medal*

**"Nothing takes the bloom off the rose of
life any more than a little pain every day."**

**"Anger is an emotion that should never
come between a doctor and a patient."**

**"The only absolute in medicine is that there are
no absolutes in medicine."**

Roman DeSanctis was born and raised in Arizona and attended the University of Arizona, where he was a star basketball player. He graduated from Harvard Medical School with honors in 1955 and began his career as a medical resident at the MGH, where he has tirelessly served for over five decades. He was appointed professor of Medicine in 1974 and subsequently was awarded the inaugural Evelyn and James Jenks–Paul Dudley White Professorship in Medicine in 1998.

First and foremost, Roman is a consummate clinician who has spent his professional life devoted to the personalized care of his patients, who have come from around the world to seek his unique expertise. He has served as a role model as a clinician, an educator, a clinical investigator, and – most importantly – an inspirational person for the past five decades. He also loves a good pun and is unrivaled as an after dinner speaker.

Roman has also devotedly served the MGH in numerous administrative roles including director of the Coronary Care Unit (1967–1981), director of Clinical Cardiology (1981–1998), and acting chief of Cardiology (1989-1991). He is currently the emeritus director of Clinical Cardiology.

In recognition of his many contributions, he was awarded the Trustees Medal (2007) by the Mass General Physicians Organization. Comments at that ceremony included "... he is the single best physician at MGH" and "... his talents at the bedside are unrivaled."

During the past 30 years, Roman has been extraordinarily committed to philanthropy. He established a professorship at Harvard Medical School and developed the Clinical Scholars Program within the Cardiology Division. He is now committed to establishing the Fund for Clinical Excellence.

Among his greatest legacies will be his lifelong commitment to inspiring and training future generations of clinician-scientists and educators. For more than five decades, there has been only one "Roman" at MGH. He continues to set the standard for excellence in everything that he does and his legacy will be far reaching.

Biographical note prepared by G. William Dec, Jr., MD

■ W. Hardy Hendren, MD

**"Dr. Hardy Hendren was a great teacher of
technique, and taught me to let the little finger
of my operating hand touch the retractor
or some fixed object, which virtually eliminated
all tremor in your operating hand,
which I still use today."**

— *submitted by Melvin Platt, MD*

**"Military flying has many of the same requisites
as being a surgeon including self discipline,
long training, stamina, attention to small details,
rapid decision-making and working in harmony
with others to get the job done right."**

**"In the operating room if you say, 'that looks good enough,'
it probably isn't good enough."**

**"I know you want to see, but if you
don't hold on to the retractor,
neither one of us can see."**

W. Hardy Hendren, one of the leading pediatric surgeons and educators of his time, was renowned for his pioneering ability to correct what were considered intractable anatomical conditions, specifically "megaureter," conjoined Siamese twins, cloacal defects and undiversion.

Dr. Hendren trained in Surgery at the MGH and was chief resident under the guidance of Dr. Edward D. Churchill. He then trained in pediatric surgery at Boston Children's Hospital under the famed Dr. Robert Gross, where he also encountered Dr. William E. Ladd, the father of pediatric surgery.

After his eight years of surgical training he returned to the MGH and was appointed chief of Pediatric Surgery by Dr. Churchill. Twenty years later he returned to Children's, where he was named chief of General Surgery and the

Robert Gross Professor of Surgery at Harvard Medical School. He operated on thousands of patients, many of whom had already failed conventional attempts at repair of defects, and trained a generation of pediatric surgeons.

Dr. Hendren has been the recipient of more than 35 major awards and honors, the most notable being the Henry Jacob Bigelow Medal from the Boston Surgical Society, an award given periodically to a person considered to be one of the world's most outstanding surgeons. He gave over 100 guest lectures and was a visiting professor at 38 universities abroad and on more than 40 occasions in the United States. Most included operations on the most difficult surgical patients. For example, there is one birth in 250,000 with a cloaca. Dr Hendren is currently writing a book of his experience with over 200 instances of cloacal defects.

In 2008 the Hendren Chair in Surgery was established at Harvard Medical School. Three teaching fellowships have been established in his name by grateful families whose children he cared for. Dr Hendren, considered by many to have been the world's most outstanding pediatric surgeon of his generation, is a man of stern countenance, great compassion and extraordinary commitment who persevered with pioneering efforts to produce innovations that revolutionized the practice of pediatric surgery.

Biographical note prepared by Stephen P. Dretler, MD

■ Ashby C. Moncure, MD

"I don't go on the court to lose."

Dr. Moncure, recalling an experience with Bobby Orr when he was the team physician for the Boston Bruins, submitted the following story:

"Orr, the greatest player in hockey, would always arrive before a game several hours before 'warm ups' and would be very active, planing his hockey sticks, etc. I arrived to cover the game very early one night, and Bobby Orr noted me curiously following his activities with my eyes. He ultimately came over and answered my unasked question by saying 'Doc, this game is played between the ears.' Hockey – a metaphor for life."

Dr. Moncure retired in 2011 after 48 years of service to the MGH and his patients. He was the "surgeon's surgeon" of his generation with expertise in

general, vascular and thoracic surgery. He would frequently be called to the OR by other surgeons who had run into difficulty and his arrival was frequently accompanied by a sigh of relief from the operating surgeon.

At his retirement dinner, Dr. Andrew Warshaw, who was hosting the affair, asked the 250 guests to stand if they had been operated on by Dr. Moncure. Approximately one third of those assembled stood. Dr. Warshaw then asked the audience still sitting to stand if they had arranged for Dr. Moncure to see or operate on a close relative. The remainder of the guests stood and the entire room then remained standing, according Dr. Moncure a lengthy and vigorous ovation.

Biographical note prepared by Willard M. Daggett, MD, and Stephen P. Dretler, MD

■ W. Gerald Austen, MD

**"It is very important always to be truthful.
It is the right thing to do, and in addition,
you don't have to remember what you said,"**
— paraphrasing Mark Twain

**"Before you go to war, make sure the
battle is worth winning."**

An honors graduate of Massachusetts Institute of Technology and Harvard Medical School, Dr. Austen trained in surgery at the MGH and was appointed chief of Cardiac Surgery at MGH in 1965. He made major contributions to improving cardio-pulmonary bypass surgery, aortic dissection treatment, and cardiac valve surgery. He also developed novel circulatory support systems for the failing heart. At the age of 36, he was one of the youngest individuals to be promoted to the rank of full professor at HMS.

Austen became chief of Surgery at MGH in 1969 at the age of 39 and held that title as well as the Edward D. Churchill Professorship for almost 29 years, until the end of 1997. During his tenure he created a very successful full time group practice in surgery and also instituted a new system of surgical divisions in the department with each division having its own chief. The Department of Surgery flourished under his leadership.

Dr. Austen continues as the Edward D. Churchill Distinguished Professor of Surgery, chair of the Chief's Council and honorary trustee at MGH. Honoring his prodigious career and outstanding philanthropic accomplishments at MGH, the five floors in the new Lunder Building devoted to patient care were named the W. Gerald Austen, MD, Inpatient Care Pavilion.

Biographical note prepared by Willard M. Daggett, MD

■ Richard H. Sweet, MD

"The relative success or failure of any surgical procedure lies in attention to what may on first thought appear to be unimportant, small details."

THE SWEET ROOM

Dedicated to the Surgeons of the
Massachusetts General Hospital.
Here is preserved our past,
generated our present and planned our future.
Here are memorialized those attributes
of a great surgeon; maturity of judgement,
dexterity of hand, devotion in teaching,
and serenity in crisis, so well exemplified by

RICHARD H. SWEET, M.D.
Visiting Surgeon 1942 - 1961

"Master among Masters" were the words chosen by Dr. Edward D. Churchill in his eulogy of Richard H. Sweet, who died while in office as president of The American Association for Thoracic Surgeons.

A graduate of the East Surgical Service in 1930, he soon became interested in thoracic surgery. He believed that surgery in this field should be based on skill in general surgery. He often used the Wellington saying that the Battle of Waterloo was won on the playing fields of Eton. His parallel: struggles in the chest are won in skills developed in the pelvis. He was a pioneer in surgery of the chest. His textbook *Thoracic Surgery* (1950) rests in the National Medical Library in Washington, DC.

He was unassuming but confident, patient but critical, and soft spoken but emphatic. He inspired the utmost respect from his residents; to them he was Sir Richard. He had a penchant for wearing red ties and was known to a few as The Cardinal. He always wore a full suit making rounds with his vest notable for its gold chain with his AOA key.

But above all, perpetuated by the inscription outside *his* room he is best remembered with these words: those attributes of a great surgeon; maturity of judgement, dexterity of hand, devotion in teaching, and serenity in crisis.

A true pioneer with these talents is perhaps unique.

Biographical note prepared by E. Wayne Wilkins, Jr., MD

Cary W. Akins, MD

"You shine brighter in reflected light."

"Don't ask for someone else's opinion unless you are willing to listen to it."

Although it was a quarter of a century ago, I can still vividly remember the first time I saw Cary Akins perform heart surgery. I was a new, bright-eyed but terrified junior resident on the "Big Red Machine." Never before and never since have I been more impressed by a surgical operation. At first, I was struck by the speed of his hands. It was unbelievable how fast Cary could cut, sew and tie. Even more astounding than Cary's speed was the fact that every incision and stitch was exact, precise and perfect. Cary was an amazing heart surgeon. He was recognized around the world for his expertise in the surgical management of coronary artery disease, valvular heart disease, mitral valve repair and aortic root replacement. Over the next several years, I came to appreciate that Cary was more than a gifted technical surgeon. In fact, his hands had a difficult time keeping up with his brain. He was a dedicated cardiac surgical scholar, a clinical researcher and a prolific writer who published numerous articles on surgical techniques and results. Cary was an active contributor to journals and a highly respected member of the cardiothoracic surgical societies.

Cary's impact on surgical resident education was profound. We all spent many months on the cardiac service and much of that time was with Cary. It was among our most formative rotations. There was no one in my general surgical training who taught me more about surgery. He taught me how to plan and execute an operation with efficiency and precision. He was as capable at the bedside as he was in the operating room. Cary always knew everything about the patient and his or her disease and peri-operative management. He taught us how to approach sick patients using an organized and systematic method. Like all great MGH surgeons Cary possessed total commitment and he lived by the credo: "attention to detail." He demanded excellence from himself and all those who helped take care of his patients. What might seem like a stressful situation to the uninitiated was actually a surgical rite of passage: to recount stories of your "Cary time" at the 9:00 O'clock Meal. It was a source of laughs, pride and growth.

When I finished my training and joined the MGH staff, Cary was a welcoming colleague and supportive partner. He was always available and willing, if asked, to offer advice on a complex patient or problem. Like his surgery and patient care, Cary's opinions were always thoughtful, detailed and exact.

Cary has many talents and gifts. He is a voracious reader of history and an avid automobile enthusiast. Although hard to imagine, Cary may be more talented as a painter than he was as a heart surgeon. Outside of the MGH, Cary's support of the Boston Health Care for the Homeless Program has been recognized by the dedication of the Cary W. Akins Pavilion at BHCHP's new inpatient and outpatient health center.

Biographical note prepared by Thomas E. MacGillivray, MD

SIGN LANGUAGE

Sign posted in one of the MGH operating rooms:

"If it is difficult you are
not doing it right."

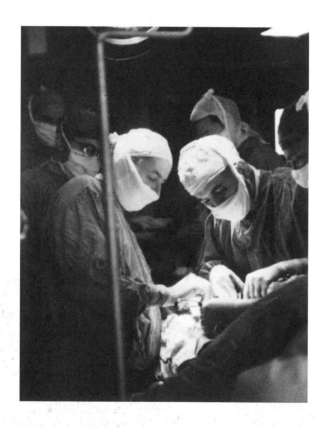

■ Allan L. Friedlich, MD

"This is the worst case I have ever seen of whatever it was."

— upon encountering a patient with a complicated and alarming course for which no diagnosis was forthcoming, and who recovered spontaneously

Born in DesMoines, Iowa, on April 24, 1917, Dr. Allan L. Friedlich graduated from Dartmouth College summa cum laude in 1939 and from Harvard Medical magna cum laude in 1943. After three years in the Air Force in World War II, he joined the staff of the MGH in 1952. Dr. Friedlich went on to develop an international reputation as a consulting cardiologist. He was a

co-director of the MGH's first cardiac catheterization laboratory. He loved the practice of medicine and was a superb physician who prided himself on taking meticulous and highly personal care of his patients. For his entire career he served as a mentor and teacher to scores of young trainees in medicine and cardiology, many of whom went on to assume major leadership positions in academic medicine. He had a wonderful sense of humor and was a great raconteur. He had a trove of marvelously funny stories about his "Uncle George," who was George S. Kaufman, the famous playwright and savant. Dr. Friedlich retired from the MGH in 1997 and passed away in 2006.

Biographical note prepared by Roman W. DeSanctis, MD

■ Paul S. Russell, MD

"You don't transplant patients; you transplant organs into patients."

Dr. Russell would typically respond with these words to the intern on rounds who had just announced, "We transplanted Mrs. G last night."

Paul was born in Chicago and received his Bachelor of Philosophy, Bachelor of Science and MD degrees from the University of Chicago. Paul then came to the MGH for his surgical training and in 2013 was recognized for his 65th year of service to the institution.

Paul was appointed MGH chief of Surgery in 1962. In addition to running the Surgical Service, Paul established an unusually productive transplantation surgery/immunology laboratory where over the next five decades he trained many of the leaders in the field and made numerous seminal contributions. These include: helping to elucidate the immunosuppressive properties of antilymphocyte sera, understanding the antigenicity of the trophoblast, undertaking early clinical trials of marrow transplantation for the treatment of leukemia and developing microsurgical models for organ transplantation in mice. He continually worked at the interface between basic science and clinical applications and held the respect of his colleagues in both arenas. He is a devoted and respected teacher and a stalwart of The Transplantation Society, which he helped to found and of which he was the fifth president.

In 1990, Paul ostensibly retired. At his festschrift, Dr. Tom Starzl summarized Paul's career most succinctly when he stated "… all the while your profile grew of the surgeon/scientist, the Socratic educator surrounded by students from three generations, the disciplined investigator with brilliant insight into murky problems, and the Bostonian gentleman." However, Paul really didn't retire and he continues his many active roles at the MGH and HMS, particularly as a teacher whose sage advice:

"Always listen to the patient; and, if the patient is a child, listen to the mother"

is still the key despite the development of advanced technologic diagnostics.

Most recently, Paul chaired the MGH History Committee, where he almost single-handedly inspired and oversaw construction of the Museum of Medical History and Innovation named in his honor.

Biographical note prepared by A. Benedict Cosimi, MD

■ Leland S. McKittrick, MD

"You shouldn't operate when the patient is getting better and you shouldn't operate when the patient is getting worse."

— *response from Arthur Allen, MD:*

"Well, Leland, you must not be operating much these days."

McKittrick was a much respected senior member of the MGH surgical staff in the nineteen forties and fifties. A "general surgeon," he had wide interests and made contributions to the care of such difficult problems as acute ulcerative colitis, cancer of the colon and duodenal ulcer disease. Working at a time when no scan imaging or even arteriograms were available, his clinical management of diabetic vascular disease of the lower extremity was particularly celebrated as it saved many patients from more extensive amputations. He worked both at the MGH and the Joslin Clinic and was renowned as a teacher and ethical clinician of the highest order. The quote above was said to be a remark he made at surgical rounds that prompted the reply from Arthur Allen, an equally august surgeon.

Biographical note prepared by Paul S. Russell, MD

Wyland F. Leadbetter, MD

"You can be in and out of a room quickly on daily rounds, but at one time during a patient's hospitalization you must stop, sit in a chair, and talk with the patient."

Dr. Leadbetter, a Phi Beta Kappa graduate of Bates College and an AOA graduate of Johns Hopkins Medical School, was a urologic surgeon of world

renown who was chief of Urology at the MGH from 1954 to 1969. He was loved by his patients and held in highest esteem by his residents and students, who came from around the world to observe him operate and care for his patients. Dr. Leadbetter was one of the first generation of urologists trained by Dr. Hugh Hampton Young. His commitment to teaching resulted in many of his residents going on to become department chairs and leaders in urology in the United States.

His work ethic was legendary. "The Boss," as he was known by his residents, worked seven days a week. Six days a week he fulfilled his duties at the MGH and on Sundays he conducted rounds at the Boston Veterans Hospital.

Each morning he rose at 4:30am, ate a hearty breakfast, walked from his home on Marlborough Street in the Back Bay, arrived to meet his residents in the White Lobby promptly at 6am and made rounds on 30 to 60 patients for two hours. At 8am he went to the operating room, where he toiled until 6 to 7pm on complex surgical problems, then went to his office in the same building to see outpatients for an hour. At 7pm he walked home, had his dinner and arrived back at the hospital for evening rounds by 9pm. For his evening rounds (unlike the 6am rounds) his patients were awake, the rooms were lit and he took the time to pull up a chair and sit and talk with his patients and their families. It was at evening rounds that his patients got to revere him.

Biographical note prepared by Stephen P. Dretler, MD

Stephen P. Dretler, MD

"If the wife says the patient doesn't look well ... he doesn't."

"Invent yourself out of business – then be ready for the next thing."

Stephen Paul Dretler, MD, arrived at the MGH in 1965 (49 years ago), where he began his surgical, and then urology, residency. Steve served in the United States Air Force for two years as chief of Surgery in South Carolina. He then returned to the MGH to complete his residency and was recruited to join the Urology department in 1972.

The United States had landed men on the moon; however, major open surgery was the standard of care for kidney and ureteral stones that could not pass. Dr. Dretler changed the paradigm on kidney stone management. As a doctor/scientist, Steve researched the chemical and physical properties of kidney stones. He was tireless in his pursuit of understanding every aspect of human kidney stone disease from basic science to the development of minimally invasive outpatient procedures. In 1972 Steve received the prestigious First Prize Clinical Research Award of the American Urologic Association.

Along his innovative journey Steve maintained his commitment to academic and surgical teaching. With Steve Dretler, there was no missing link between basic science and treatment. He produced multiple educational videos for which he received The Gold Medal Award from the International Film and TV Festival in New York in 1988.

Steve studied the physical properties of kidney stones and their matrix. Understanding the physical properties led him to do collaborative research with laser physicists at the MGH Wellman Laboratory to develop a laser capable of fragmenting a stone into grains of sand. He then popularized the mini-ureteroscope, a tiny scope capable of passage into the ureter without dilating the ureteral tunnel as a vehicle both to visualize the stone and to carry the newly invented laser fiber. In essence, this was early natural orifice surgery. I was Steve's resident at this time and experienced the quantum change in stone management.

Steve's perseverance led him to look for further minimally invasive treatments for stone disease, including very early work with Extracorporeal Shock Wave Lithotripsy (ESWL). Steve developed the MGH ESWL Stone Center, one of the earliest in the U.S.

Dr. Dretler was the first to understand the variable fragility of stones and published numerous articles to educate physicians on optimal treatments for kidney stones, not just by size but also by their fragility (tendency to break) with various energy sources. He even coined new words – "durile" and "durility" – to describe a stone's level of fragility.

While being a great surgeon, teacher and mentor, Steve defines what it is to be a reliable friend. He is always available to give medical as well as life advice and cares about the residents' well being in life. Steve has been a mentor to three decades of urology residents.

Biographical note prepared by Francis J. McGovern, MD

■ Walter C. Guralnick, DMD

"So you think you are all so important. Let me ask you this. If all of the oral surgical interns and all sanitation workers in Boston went on strike at the same time, whom would the people be begging to return to work first?"

— *Walter C. Guralnick, DMD, speaking to a group of rambunctious, newly graduated oral maxillofacial surgical interns*

"Surgery is a practice as much for the mind as for the hands."

Walter C. Guralnick graduated from the Massachusetts State College in 1937 and from the Harvard School of Dental Medicine in 1941. He completed residency in Oral Surgery at the Boston City Hospital and served in the U.S. Army from 1942 to 1946. While a part time faculty member he made important contributions to the understanding and management of tooth transplantation and infections. He became head of the Department of Oral Surgery at Harvard and chief of the service at the MGH in 1967 and made major advances to the specialty and dentistry. He served as president of the Massachusetts Dental Society in 1968 and was instrumental in the creation of Delta Dental Insurance in 1966. As chairman of the national oral surgery association's Committee on Residency Training he led important changes in the program requirements and evaluation including creation of an In-Service Examination. In 1971 he introduced the oral and maxillofacial surgery MD general surgery program at Harvard and the MGH. This program has been emulated throughout the U.S. since then. He is a member of the Institute of Medicine and has received numerous awards including the Harvard University Alumni Gold Medal in 2005. In the 1980s he was an early ambassador for Project Hope in China. Although he stepped down from his clinical and academic roles in 1981, he served the MGH as director of the Ambulatory Care Center and then director of the Operating Rooms. The Walter Guralnick Endowed Chair in Oral and Maxillofacial Surgery was created in 1992 and honors his legacy and achievements. He remains an active member of the community today.

Biographical note prepared by R. Bruce Donoff, MD

■ Leslie W. Ottinger, MD

"Surgery is a humbling and, at times, humiliating specialty."

"In truth, tired and knowledgeable is considerably more to the patient's advantage than rested and ignorant."

"Patients do better if you worry about them."

Dr. Ottinger, an honors graduate of Rice University, spent three years as a line officer in the U.S. Navy and graduated from Harvard Medical School. He came to the MGH as a surgical intern in 1960, finishing his training as East resident (chief resident) in

1966. Following that he served on the surgical staff of the MGH and faculty of Harvard Medical School until he retired in 1996. Among other contributions to the surgical literature, he published numerous articles on mesenteric vascular lesions and authored a book on colon surgery.

For 30 years the program director of the MGH general surgical residency, Dr. Ottinger was devoted to the training and well being of MGH resident surgeons. An accomplished surgeon in his own right, he consistently strove to assist the residents, one on one, in attaining that same degree of clinical mastery. He was honored in 2012 by the establishment of the Ferguson/Ottinger Visiting Professorship and Fund for the support of surgical residents.

Biographical note prepared by Willard M. Daggett, MD

Peter R. Mueller, MD

"Every procedure must be performed with the same diligence and meticulousness no matter how simple it appears. This is because what sometimes looks like a simple case turns out to be difficult and what looks complicated initially turns out to be simple. The saving grace in managing all of these 'easy and hard' cases is sticking to the basic principles of interventional radiology."

"Easy is hard, hard is easy."

As an avid golfer Dr. Mueller recognized that the phrase "chip shot" was not as easily accomplished as is often implied on the golf course. Transposing this concept to his approaches to interventional radiology, he invoked this thought to a host of younger staff members. This attitude reinforced to them that focused concentration, planning and execution are crucial to the success of all interventional procedures.

After graduating from Harvard and the University of Cincinnati Medical School, Peter joined the staff of the department's Gastrointestinal Imaging Division following completion of his residency in 1974. He quickly recognized that the newly employed cross sectional imaging techniques created the capacity to develop precise interventional procedures in the abdomen. He proceeded to introduce percutaneous procedures such as abscess drainage, biliary drainage, gastrostomy and most recently percutaneous tumor ablation methods at the MGH. He became director of the newly renamed Division of Abdominal Imaging and Interventional Radiology in 1989 and remained its leader for almost 25 years. He became professor of Radiology in 1999 and currently is the director of Interventional Radiology throughout the department. Many of his fellows have gone on to assume major interventional directorships both nationally and internationally.

Biographical note prepared by Jack Wittenberg, MD

■ Charles J. McCabe, MD

"Your job in the Emergency Department is to create order out of chaos."

"Don't trade technology for good clinical skills."

"Death begins in Radiology."

I came to the MGH in 1995 and by then Dr. McCabe was a pre-eminent professor of surgery. As an emergency neuroradiologist, I was fortunate to work with Charlie on many challenging cases and was honored to help him on many occasions to understand his own condition (MS) by reviewing his imaging with him. Charlie had a good sense of humor, keen clinical skills and a deep sense of compassion for his patients that he conveyed not only to his students but also to all who worked with him. He would often advise his students (and me, in jest) that "Death begins in Radiology." Although this admonition sounds initially harsh, his point was clear. Very sick patients coming into the emergency room above all require the acumen of a skilled diagnostician at the bedside. Technology affords us many advantages, but one should not be quick to shuttle a critical patient out of the immediate care of the clinical team to take advantage of an imaging study that only serves to augment what can already be ascertained from a careful clinical examination.

— *submitted by Thomas Ptak, MD*

These are some of the numerous "Charlieisms" - irreverent but unforgettable statements by Dr. Charles J. McCabe. "CJ," "Charlie" or just plain "Doc," as he was known, was in his youth a phenomenal athlete. After completing his residency in surgery at the MGH, he entered the Cardiothoracic Training Program, but on the cusp of graduation, illness in the shape of multiple sclerosis forced him to accept a different calling - that of teaching the medical students and residents the science, the art, and the humanity of surgery. Every morning at 6:30am he would hold court in the Emergency Department and review the surgical cases that had been evaluated over the previous 24 hours. Woe betides the resident who sent an unstable patient for additional testing when the patient should have gone straight to the operating room. Once admonished in this manner, this was a lifelong learned experience. It is no coincidence that, to this day, the teaching award at HMS is the Charles McCabe Award.

Biographical note prepared by Alasdair K. Conn, MD

Misha L. Pless, MD

"You might get a Doctor of Arts in four years, but it will take you 40 to learn the art of doctoring."

Dr. Misha Luis Pless was born in Cochabamba, Bolivia. He received his undergraduate degree in chemistry and history from Stanford University and his medical degree from Emory University. He completed his medical internship at the MGH in 1990, followed by residency in Neurology at the Brigham & Women's Hospital and fellowship in Neuro-Ophthalmology at the Massachusetts Eye & Ear Infirmary. He was then recruited to the

University of Pittsburgh School of Medicine, where he flourished as a neurologist and neuro-ophthalmologist. He returned to Boston in 2004 and, after a brief foray into private practice, joined the Neurology faculty at MGH. In 2012, he began a two-year leave to work in Switzerland.

A renowned expert in neuro-ophthalmology, multiple sclerosis, neuro-inflammation and general neurology, Dr. Pless is also well known to the MGH medical community for his kindness, his generosity and his availability to assist other physicians in the management of

neurologic problems. He is legendary for answering emails at all hours of the day or night to help triage a case to its proper destination, or avert the need for an unnecessary test.

Dr. Pless is fluent in multiple languages, and is a lover of the arts, music and culture from around the world. He brings this appreciation for the arts to his daily life and to his interactions with colleagues and with patients. He knows and appreciates the benefits of years of aging and maturation that a fine wine experiences in the barrel, and thus it is utterly fitting that his perspective on the process of making a great doctor so clearly parallels that sentiment.

Biographical note prepared by Lee H. Schwamm, MD

■ Leigh H. Simmons, MD

"You should never worry alone."

This statement guides a collaborative to patient care and originated in the Psychiatry Department.

A graduate of Vanderbilt University School of Medicine, Dr. Leigh H. Simmons trained in internal medicine at MGH and served as a chief resident in Medicine. She has the distinction of being the first ambulatory chief resident. Like other chief residents at MGH she is an exceptional teacher and mentor, but as ambulatory chief she added an emphasis on longitudinal and holistic care that has set the standard for others to follow. She currently practices medicine in Internal Medicine Associates at MGH, where she focuses on the care of the medically complex patient.

Leigh recalls that she heard early in her training from the psychiatry faculty the advice to "never worry alone." She found that this advice applied in many situations and uses this when mentoring residents, in consulting with colleagues about difficult cases and with patients to encourage them to share concerns in clinical consultations.

Her research interests include patient engagement in care and shared decision-making. In her role as physician fellow at the John D. Stoeckle Center for Primary Care Innovation she studies the use of decision aids to help patients and clinicians in the shared decision-making process.

In addition to her clinical and research interests, Dr. Simmons serves as a medical student educator and directs the internal medicine clerkship for Harvard Medical School students at MGH.

Biographical note prepared by Blair W. Fosburgh, MD

■ Daniel P. Hunt, MD

Dan Hunt, one of the clinician educators on the medical service, told me in a slow Texas drawl that

"the acute discovery of a chronic problem does not make the problem acute"

when asking me about why we had tried to correct something overnight on a patient who had not seen a doctor in years.

— submitted by William J. Hucker, MD, PhD

When I first met Dan Hunt in Texas almost 20 years ago, I asked him why he chose the field of medicine. Without hesitation he replied

"because it keeps you humble."

Many years later, he continues to live and practice medicine by the same credo that he inculcates in all his trainees:

"... be driven by an unquenchable desire to learn and be willing to admit humbly to limitations of knowledge."

Dan graduated from Vanderbilt University School of Medicine in 1981. After practicing medicine in a prestigious private group in Houston for eleven years, he joined the teaching faculty at Baylor College of Medicine in 1995 as a full-time member of the Ben Taub General Hospital staff. Over the ensuing years he would become one of the most celebrated and decorated teaching faculty members in BCM history.

He then joined MGH and Harvard Medical School, where he had been avidly recruited to direct the newly created Inpatient Clinician Educator Service at MGH. Since his arrival he has been the recipient of the prestigious Alfred Kranes Teaching Award twice in the department of Medicine at MGH and of the Best Clinical Teacher Award by the graduating class of 2008 at HMS. He became chief of the Hospital Medicine Unit at MGH in 2011, combining his outstanding teaching, administrative and humanistic abilities in directing this new unit.

At the national level, Dan has served on numerous major education and leadership committees. He is a clinical expert in the fields of venous thromboembolism and perioperative medicine. For his lifelong accomplishments in education he was honored with the 2011 Society of Hospital Medicine Excellence in Teaching Award.

Biographical note prepared by Alberto Puig, MD, PhD

■ G. Octo Barnett, MD

"If the most conscientious physician were to attempt to keep up with the literature by reading two articles per day, in one year even this individual would be more than 800 years behind."

"There's no such thing as 'free' text."

— referring to the importance of using structured data fields in electronic medical records

A graduate of Vanderbilt and Harvard Medical School, Dr. Barnett trained in cardiology at the Peter Bent Brigham Hospital before he came to the MGH and founded the Laboratory of Computer Science in 1964, one of the nation's first medical informatics research divisions. As professor of Medicine at HMS and division chief for almost 40 years, he and his teams made internationally-renowned contributions to the nascent fields of medical informatics and health information technology, including the MUMPS (now M) programming language used widely in health care; COSTAR, one of the first ambulatory electronic medical records that presciently supported structured notes and a problem-based record; DXplain, a diagnostic decision support system; and more. He mentored and trained many of the current leaders in the field, and instilled them with his philosophy that free-form text in clinical narratives is cheap to collect but expensive to use in ways that improve health outcomes.

Dr. Barnett is a member of the Institute of Medicine and a founding fellow and former president of the American College of Medical Informatics, ultimately receiving its Morris Collen Award of Excellence, the highest honor bestowed by the college.

Biographical note prepared by Henry Chueh, MD, MS

Alfred Kranes, MD, examining a patient in the Ether Dome

TEACHING AND TRAINING

■ Daniel D. Federman, MD

"Stick to basics.
Think out loud.
Be kind."

— Federman's mantra for clinical teaching

Dan Federman lived his mantra – he understood the basics of all aspects of medicine, he exposed us all to his reasoning process, and he was forever kind (and forgiving). But for those of us who wanted to "be like Dan" (and there were many), we came to realize that there is more to the Federman magic than these three principles, as important as they are. The magic comes from a prodigious intellect that is able to make complex subjects understandable, an unparalleled verbal skill, and an incomparable understanding of human nature. He sets a high standard that we all continue to try to reach. He and his late wife Betty (a former Bulfinch head nurse) lived and breathed the MGH, and they represented its essence in many ways.

Biographical note prepared by George E. Thibault, MD, the first Daniel D. Federman Professor of Medicine and Medical Education at Harvard Medical School

■ Robert A. Hughes, MD

**"Always think out loud.
Never be afraid to ask a question.
Never worry alone.
Always be kind."**

*— Hughes' teaching mantra (obviously, but unknowingly, passed down
within the MGH by Dr. Federman and other colleagues)*

**"Always remember that you are your own most important
patient. If you do not take care of yourself – physically, mentally
and spiritually – you can not take care of anybody else."**

The last quote is one Dr. Hughes says he took to heart from Dr. Walter
St. Goar, an MGH clinical mentor, when he was a resident.

Bob Hughes played quarterback at his high school and went to Harvard,
where he played defensive back for two years. He says he learned about
teams, about how the team is only as strong as the weakest member and
must work together, and,

**"Clinical medicine is a team sport played by doctors, nurses
and administrators and anyone who thinks it's just about
doctors is missing two-thirds of the picture."**

Bob has been a builder of programs – the
game plans and teams to make them work.
From residency in 1982 he was asked to
take leadership of the Anticoagulation
Management Service, and in 1985 the
Massachusetts Eye and Ear Infirmary asked
him to run their Medical Consult Service. In
1990, he put together the Bulfinch Medical
Group.

When asked why he only played two years
in college, Bob says that as a QB he liked
to call the plays, but as a DB he just got beat up. In his career as a leader of
programs he gets both to call the plays *and* get beat up.

Biographical note prepared by Charles H. Weiss, MD

THE MGH ANESTHESIA INTERVIEW

by Gilles Chambob, MD

I was interviewing for a fellowship in Critical Care Medicine at the MGH.
I was invited to the MGH, and I found myself sitting in a dimly lit room with
Roger Wilson, Dick Teplick, Bart Chernow, William Hurford, Warren Zapol
and several others whom I don't recall now. (All of these men had enormous
stature.) It was somewhat intimidating to say the least. We got through the
initial pleasantries and my background. Then one of them asked, "Well now
we know your background, but what can you offer the MGH?" I was a
28-year-old anesthesia resident from N.Y. A simple MD with no research
background, no PhD, no Nobel Prize in Medicine. Not even a Navy Seal.
I thought that any accolades that I had were puny relative to what those
gentlemen had seen. So I figured there was no use telling them about my
brilliant anesthesia scores at the ABA or, even less so, my athletic abilities. So
I said, "Donuts." "I beg your pardon" was the response of one giant gentleman
sitting across from me. "Donuts," I meekly repeated. There was a silence, and
then they all laughed. I broke the ice and the rest of the interview was a piece
of cake. I was in.

■ Warren M. Zapol, MD

When Warren was chair and I was his vice-chair, he used to remind me:

"Take care of your people. They take care of us."

— *submitted by Robert C. Schneider, MD*

Warren M. Zapol: intensivist, scientist, innovator. BS MIT (1962);
MD University of Rochester School of Medicine (1966). Reginald Jenney
Professor of Anaesthesia, HMS (1991). His career is dedicated to lessening
the suffering of the sick, expanding the horizon of medicine and science, and
supporting and fostering the careers of his fellow physicians and scientists.

His academic life is marked by firsts. He helped develop the use of extended
extracorporeal circulation at NIH then proved its usefulness for life-threatening

acute lung injury. He moved
the study of seal physiology
and biochemistry from the
laboratory to free-swimming seals,
envisioning the use of underwater
computer recording and blood
sampling. He pioneered the use of
nitric oxide in acute lung injury,
persistent fetal circulation, sickle
cell crises and, most recently,
cerebral malaria.

He was elected to the Institute of
Medicine (2002) and was twice
appointed to the U.S. Antarctic
Research Commission (2008,
2012). As chair of the department
of Anesthesia and Critical Care (1994–2008), he reinvigorated its research
mission and expanded it to study the role of neuroplasticity in pain;
enlarged the clinical department despite predictions of a diminished
need for anesthesiologists; and endowed four new department chairs.
He stepped down as chair to resume full-time research, where he
continues his groundbreaking work.

Biographical note prepared by Robert C. Schneider, MD

THE MGH SURGICAL INTERN INTERVIEW

by Melvin R. Platt, MD

The interview was quite important to me as a non-Ivy graduate trying to decide whether I would even be considered for the MGH residency despite being first in my class. I was sent to interview with Dr. George Nardi, who was very gracious and encouraging to me, but I'll never forget what he said to me when trying to describe the committee system to select the intern class. He told me I would be asked "everything from the branches of the aorta to my latest experience at a house of ill repute," but if you knew George, he used a much less politically correct term for the end of that phrase. Needless to say, I applied and got in, and eventually became the East chief, and though I was prepared to answer the proposed question, it was never asked.

During my "senior committee" oral session, I felt I had done very well, especially with the last question asked by a bald-headed gentleman whom I didn't know at the time (Linton), who asked me the distinctions between Buerger's disease and atherosclerosis. Being from Baylor, where DeBakey wrote the book on Buerger's disease, I carefully listed the differences between the two entities. I walked out proud as a peacock, only to run into Al Cohen (a Harvard Medical senior and soon to be a fellow intern), who informed me that Dr. Linton did not believe there was such a thing as Buerger's disease. I sulked all the way back to Houston, only to be accepted anyway, so I guess they accepted my enthusiasm over my knowledge.

WHAT, YOU DID NOT GO TO HARVARD?

by James Callison, MD

I went to Vanderbilt medical school and could not apply to the MGH internship because I could not afford transportation from Nashville to Boston. In the spring, after the internship assignments, I was able to visit the MGH and inquire about residency. I was told that the MGH did not take new residents as all the interns stayed for residency. In February I was called and told that one of the interns decided to go into surgical pathology making an opening in the program. Of course I took it. Dr. Ed Hamlin, when I was scrubbing with him, said "I don't remember you as an intern." "No I interned at Vanderbilt." "What, you did not go to Harvard? You did not intern here? What are you doing here now?"

■ H. Thomas Ballantine, Jr., MD

H. Thomas Ballantine, MD, an MGH neurosurgeon who
graduated from Johns Hopkins, when often asked,
"When did you graduate from Harvard?" would say,

"I didn't graduate from Harvard, I just came here to teach."

H. Thomas Ballantine, Jr., Princeton 1933, John Hopkins School of Medicine
MD 1937, MGH 1938, left to serve in the North Africa Combat Zone

preparatory to the invasion of
Sicily. Following neurosurgical
training at the University
of Michigan he joined the
neurosurgical staff at MGH
in 1947. He was among the
first in conjunction with the
Acoustics Laboratory and Leo
Beranek at MIT to explore the
use of focused ultrasound to
ablate mass lesions. In addition
he studied surgical approaches
to the spine and the use of
cingulotomy for chronic pain
and disabling psychiatric illness.

He was a trustee of the
American Medical Association.
He founded the Commonwealth
Institute of Medicine to further his mission to expose "quackery" and ethical
breaches in medicine. This led to his appointment by President Ronald Reagan
to the President's Commission for the Study of Ethical Problems in Medicine
and Biomedical and Behavioral Research.

In 1969 he received an honorary DSc degree from Suffolk University.
In 1983 he was promoted to clinical professor of Surgery at HMS.
Tom Ballantine was a wonderful mentor and a loyal colleague.

Biographical note prepared by Nicholas T. Zervas, MD

THE INTERN'S STEP

by Peter G. Barrett, MD

Mr. Bulfinch made a mistake. Close attention to the south stairways leading from the lawn into the first floor of the Bulfinch building will reveal that the height of the top step is one-and-a-half inches greater than the lower dozen steps. In the 1960s, anxious interns with clean, pressed, white uniforms hurried up the stairs each week on their way to teaching conferences. Early in the academic year, some of them would misjudge the top step and trip, scattering charts, papers and stethoscopes everywhere. All occurred within the view and the sound of the house staff and faculty who were gathered inside the nearby conference room. Dr. Dwight Robinson gave me lots of useful advice and one bit of it saved me from the embarrassment of tripping on the "Intern's Step." Dr. Robinson explained that it had been called the "Intern's Step" because of the mishaps it had caused. Experienced residents never tripped on it. It is now painted red.

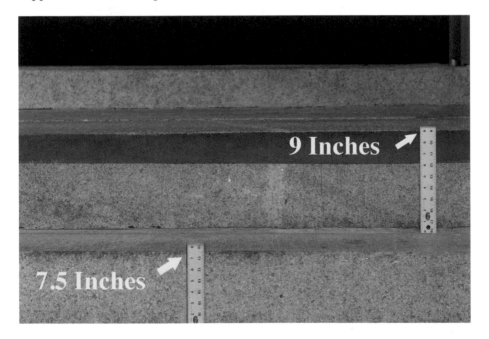

■ I. David Todres, MD

"Always sit down when you talk to patients or their families."

I. David Todres, MD, My Best Teacher

I was a pediatric resident at MGH beginning in 1975, having done my internship at Boston City, then going into the service for two years and then returning to MGH. Dr. David Todres was attending in pediatric critical care, which was my first rotation (and the most difficult) after leaving the service that very hot July.

You cannot imagine how nervous I was during the first days of my residency – these patients were critically ill. I had to intubate a premature baby, and I had not intubated anyone for more than two years. It is not what David said when he was helping me to intubate the baby – it was his manner, confidence in me, reassuring tone and extraordinary calm in the face of a potential disaster that have stayed with me over these decades. I know very well that I appreciated these characteristics in him, and I try to emulate David when I am teaching the residents here.

David was a master teacher, clinician and communicator in addition to being a brilliant man who was extraordinarily cultured and especially interested in medical ethics. Even though I did not enter neonatology or critical care, David was a profound influence on me. I am extraordinarily grateful that my office was a couple down from his in his last years. To this day, I remember his soft British accent, and that continues to warm me. Thanks for giving me the opportunity to remember him.

Biographical note prepared by Mark A. Goldstein, MD

■ Harriet L. Hardy, MD

**"Ask your patients not only their occupation
but what work they do on the job."**

Harriet L. Hardy came to the MGH in the middle of her career. She
graduated from Cornell Medical School in 1932 and served a residency
at Philadelphia General Hospital. She then worked as school physician at
Northfield Seminary, a preparatory school in Northfield, Massachusetts, and
also at Radcliffe College, from which she sought research in the Division
of Occupational Hygiene, Massachusetts Department of Labor. These new
interests led to an MGH appointment in 1945 to head an Occupational
Medicine Clinic with the support of Drs. Walter Bauer, James H. Means, and
Arlie Bock. Her work took her out of the office into factories, mines, and
laboratories to examine work hazards and into homes to interview workers,
their wives too, about their job and their health. That interest she carried into
clinical practice, and in talks and rounds she urged students and residents not
only to ask patients their occupation but what work they did on the job. With
Dr. Irving R. Tabershaw she identified beryllium disease in workers exposed
in the manufacture of fluorescent lamps.

Biographical note prepared by John D. Stoeckle, MD

John D. Crawford, MD

John D. (Jack) Crawford, MD, was the reason I became a pediatric endocrinologist and I have spent my entire career trying to be as good as he was. Although we corresponded often, I once wrote to him explicitly to thank him for what he had done to ignite my passion for pediatric endocrinology. I think I used the metaphor that he had ignited my fuse. His response (copied exactly from his email, which I still have):

"Thanks for those kind words about lighting your fuse. I never trained anyone; the most I did was let them play with matches."

— *submitted by William E. Russell, MD*

John D. (Jack) Crawford, who was born in Boston in 1920, was a graduate of Harvard College and an Alpha Omega Alpha graduate of Harvard Medical School. Aside from two years in Cambridge, England as a research fellow, he spent his entire professional career at the MGH. He was appointed professor of Pediatrics at Harvard Medical School in 1962, and was engaged creatively in the academic practice of medicine for almost 60 years. Jack was a superb teacher and clinician. He was at his desk, collaborating in new research studies, until the day he died following a massive stroke suffered on the evening of his 85th birthday. He was chief of the Endocrine Metabolic Unit of the Children's Service at MGH from 1962 to 1990.

He was one of the founding giants of pediatric endocrinology. Among his more important contributions were research and clinical studies that helped to establish rational fluid management in infants and children and therapeutic paradigms for patients with diabetes insipidus. He was among the first to use human growth hormone to treat children with growth hormone deficiency, was influential in determining the chromosomal aberrations in Prader–Willi syndrome, championed novel approaches for the treatment and prevention of burn injuries, and was an advocate and role model for the sensitive management of children with disorders of sexual differentiation. Jack had a remarkable capacity to combine thoughtful scholarship with sincere compassion in the care of every patient and family. His many trainees and colleagues around the world recognized him as a superb exemplar of a clinical investigator and academic clinician.

Biographical note prepared by Lewis B. Holmes, MD, and Lynne L. Levitsky, MD

■ William H. Sweet, MD, PhD

FAMOUS LAST WORDS:

1. **THE FIRST TIME A NEW AND VALID THOUGHT IS CONCEIVED IS THE CRITICAL MOMENT.**
2. **LOOK THOUGHTFULLY AT INDIVIDUAL NOVEL EVENTS IN YOUR EXPERIENCE, ANALYZE THEM CAREFULLY AND DECIDE IF THEY CONTAIN THE KERNEL OF A NEW CONCEPT.**
3. **THE SIGNIFICANT STEP IS THE PASSAGE FROM NO IDEA TO ONE INSTRUCTIVE INSIGHT.**

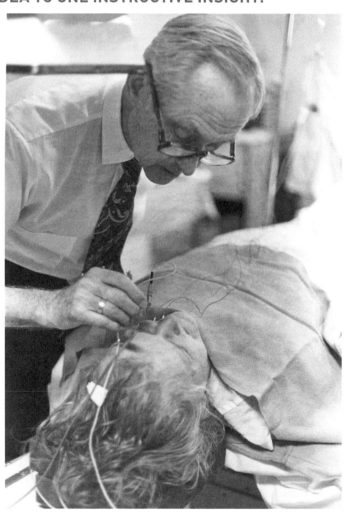

BIOGRAPHY: After receiving his DPhil from Oxford University he joined the Neurosurgical Service under Dr. James White after World War II. He was a major contributor to the fledgling field of neurosurgery, which was beginning to evolve from a disorganized and dangerous field of surgery. His interest in science was directed particularly at management of brain tumors and pain.

His major accomplishments were to gain him international recognition and served to spur others both at this hospital and in Europe and Japan. These included:

NEW UNDERSTANDING OF NEUROPHYSIOLOGY OF CSF FORMATION AND ABSORPTION

PET SCANNING FOR IMAGING OF BRAIN LESIONS

CYCLOTRON BRAGG PEAK THERAPY FOR FOCAL DESTRUCTION OF INACCESSIBLE BRAIN TUMORS

RADICAL REMOVAL OF CRANIOPHARYNGIOMA

STEREOTAXIC INSTRUMENTATION

MAJOR CONTRIBUTIONS IN CHRONIC PAIN MANAGEMENT AS CHRONICLED IN A VOLUME BY DR. WHITE AND HIMSELF

THE "HARVARD" BRAIN DEATH CRITERIA.

Biographical note prepared by Nicholas T. Zervas, MD

NEUROSURGICAL WISDOM

"Fast on the straightaways, slow on the turns."

— saying used in the neurosurgical training program, which has been passed on through the years

■ Willard M. Daggett, MD

Advice often given to surgical residents, in explaining the need to move along efficiently with the operation (and not to be overcome by obsession) is: "Better (or perfect) is the enemy of good." The origin of this aphorism, often not known to its speakers, is William Shakespeare, where in King Lear, Act One, Scene Four Albany states: "Striving to better, oft we mar what's well."

One of the statements I have often used with residents, hesitant to proceed with a procedure, paraphrases Yoda instructing Luke Skywalker on the meaning of "The Force" from The Empire Strikes Back of the Star Wars trilogy: "Either do it or don't do it, but don't tell me you'll try."

"Successful correction of ventricular fibrillation in an intensive care setting with well-trained personnel can be a routine event in an otherwise ordinary day."

Born in Wisconsin and educated at UC Berkeley, Phi Beta Kappa, and UCSF, AOA, Bill came to Boston and the MGH as a surgical intern in 1958.

He trained in surgery at MGH under Dr. Churchill and then Dr. Austen. He did research in cardiac physiology at NIH with Stanley Sarnoff and later had additional training in pediatric surgery at Children's Hospital Boston under Dr. Gross. He was the West chief resident at MGH in 1967. He became professor of Surgery at HMS in 1978.

His surgical practice developed around coarctation repairs, valves and coronaries with a particular interest in post infarction ventricular septal rupture – a group of very sick patients where Bill developed one of the world's largest and finest clinical series using generous bolts of Teflon felt to reinforce friable tissues.

In the research lab working with more than 70 fellows, Bill and his collaborator Gillian Geffin studied cardiac performance and pioneered the developing area of myocardial protection with over 25 years of NIH funding. The ultimate product of his work was cold oxygenated dilute blood cardioplegia locally known as "Daggo-plege" that enabled safe preservation of myocardial function with the long cross-clamp ischemic times that increasingly complex heart surgery required.

Bill was a determined and intensely focused surgeon, renowned for his high-powered surgical loupes, ambidexterity and sometimes-mystical pronouncements. Looking at an ICU flow sheet and gesturing into thin air far away from the top of the page, he famously admonished an ICU resident, "You're way out here on the Starling curve."

In 2008 the Divisions of Cardiac and Thoracic Surgery honored Bill with the establishment of the Willard M. Daggett Scholarship in Cardiac and Thoracic Surgical Research to support young investigators in CT surgical research.

Biographical note prepared by David F. Torchiana, MD

A LONG DAY

by Willard M. Daggett, MD

Grantly Taylor, MD, a cancer surgeon of renown and head of the Tumor Clinic at the MGH in the 1950s, brought in to the Philips House a prominent society orchestra leader for a planned resection of a recurrent sacral chordoma. Because of involvement by the tumor of the sacral neural plexus and foramina, Dr. Taylor invited Dr. William Sweet, head of Neurosurgery and a meticulous operator, to join him in the operating room. After Dr. Taylor had debulked the tumor, Dr. Sweet took over and with loop magnification carefully dissected out the involved nerves. This effort went on for several hours with Dr. Taylor sitting on a stool patiently in the corner of the room.

Finally Dr. Dwight Robinson, the surgical resident on Dr. Taylor's team, spoke up, querying:

"Dr. Sweet, have you ever had one of these tumors recur while you were operating on it?"

Dr. Taylor, doing his best to stifle laughter, fell off his stool.

The patient tolerated the lengthy procedure well.

■ Mandel E. Cohen, MD

**"The psychiatric neuroscientists are just as
bad as the Freudos – they accept completely
unsupported hypotheses."**

**"Boys, if you have a case you can't make any sense of,
then start again at the beginning and take the
history all over again."**

In the early days of carotid artery endarterectomy (1959–1960), meetings
were held with interested clinicians in the second floor Warren Building
Pathology Conference Room. At one of these meetings, Dr. Mandel Cohen
rose to comment in his thick Georgia accent:

**"You boys have shown that you can ream these arteries out
and keep 'em open; now what we need to find out is,
is it good fo' people."**

Mandel Cohen was educated at Barton
Academy in Mobile, Alabama, Yale College
in New Haven, Johns Hopkins Medical
School in Baltimore and the Harvard
Medical Service at the Boston City
Hospital in Boston.

His achievements included:

1) Performing the first cardiac
   catheterizations in New England

2) Revolutionizing psychiatric diagnosis
   through his disciples Eli and Lee Robbins,
   Sam Gaze, and others in the Washington

University School. His analyses of manic-depressive disease and anxiety
neurosis by symptoms and signs and his emphasis on data-driven psychiatric
diagnoses laid the groundwork for the Diagnostic and Statistical Manual.
He was vocally anti-Freudian. He was a member of the neurology service at
MGH until his death at age 93.

Biographical note prepared by Nicholas T. Zervas, MD

■ J. Gordon Scannell, MD

While operating as chief resident at Middlesex Tuberculosis Sanitarium in Waltham in 1965, I was blessed to have as my visit J. Gordon Scannell, with his extensive experience in surgery for tuberculosis. On one occasion early in my experience there, while carrying out an extra-pleural pneumonectomy in a patient with a destroyed left lung and recurrent tuberculous empyema, Dr. Scannell cautioned me, saying:

**"Bill, you are very good, but keep in mind,
I do not come out here to get you out of trouble."**

— *submitted by Willard M. Daggett, MD*

Gordon Scannell did the first open heart operation at the MGH to remove an atrial myxoma in 1955. He did it without cardiopulmonary bypass with hypothermia and inflow occlusion. The patient required two hours of open chest cardiac massage until his temperature could be brought up by warm pleural lavage for defibrillation. The patient did well and had a full life. Dr. Scannell was an intrepid pioneer.

Gordon Scannell lived a full life and wore many hats. Born in Boston, he attended Harvard College and wrote for the Harvard Lampoon. He was the man behind the famous incident in which the Yale mascot (a bulldog) was stolen and was subsequently photographed licking the boots of the statue of John Harvard in Harvard Yard. He went on to HMS and then the MGH.

As many of his classmates did, he contracted tuberculosis and was hospitalized for a time at a local sanitarium. He resumed his residency and was chosen by Dr. Edward D. Churchill to stay on staff. He jump started his career by studying the surgical anatomy of the lungs at the University of Minnesota and co-authored the classic papers on the surgical anatomy of the upper lobe. He was a favorite of Dr. Churchill and focused on thoracic surgery at first, then on cardiac surgery, and late in his career back on thoracic surgery again.

He was the director of the MGH Surgical Clerkship for Harvard Medical students. He became the editor of the *Harvard Medical Alumni Bulletin* and was widely recognized for his writing. He served on the American Board of Thoracic Surgery and was president of the Boston Surgical Society and the American Association for Thoracic Surgery. His joy in life outside the MGH was sailing on the Atlantic.

Biographical note prepared by Cameron D. Wright, MD

Mortimer J. Buckley, MD

"Dr. Buckley often said to residents,
'It's fun to watch the young guys coming along'
when he wasn't that happy (but not too unhappy)
with something you did."

Dr. Mortimer J. Buckley was a cardiac surgical legend at the MGH, where he spent his entire professional career. As chief of the MGH Division of Cardiac Surgery from 1970 until his retirement in 1998, Dr. Buckley was a master technician in all aspects of cardiac disease, including valvular, aortic and coronary procedures, although he felt his greatest reward lay in giving an infant an opportunity to achieve a longer, healthier life. He was relentless in his devotion to teaching residents to become cardiac surgeons, and equally demanding in what he expected in return. As a scientist, Mort was an early innovator in the application of mechanical circulatory support, especially in the development of the intra-aortic balloon pump to treat patients with acutely ischemic and failing hearts. As a capstone to his brilliant career, in 1995 he was elected president of the American Association for Thoracic Surgery.

Biographical note prepared by Cary W. Akins, MD, and Willard M. Daggett, MD

Richard J. Kitz, MD

"On my anesthesia residency exit interview I asked Dr. Kitz
what he did so well to be chair of Anesthesia working through
[the tenure of] many chairs of other departments? His reply:

'When I enter a room for critical meetings
I check my ego at the door.'

"This advice has helped me throughout my career."

— submitted by Allen J. Hinkle, MD

Richard J. Kitz, MD, is Henry Isaiah Dorr Professor of Anaesthesia Emeritus
at Harvard Medical School. A native of Oshkosh, Wisconsin, he has always
been proud of his roots. He graduated from Marquette University and did his
anesthesia training at Columbia Presbyterian Medical Center in New York,
where he was a protégé of Dr. Emanuel ("Manny") Papper.

Dick was appointed anesthetist-in-chief at
the MGH in 1969, a position he held for
a quarter century. Thereafter, he became
faculty dean for Clinical Affairs at HMS
for five years. His research focused on the
design, synthesis and testing of compounds
that provided short-acting, non-depolarizing
blockade of neuromuscular transmission.
Working with colleagues, this research led
to the introduction of several novel drugs
that were widely used clinically. Dick and
his wonderful wife, Jeanne, now reside in
Westwood, Mass.

I met Dick in 1969 when his infectious
energy, honesty and determination instantly
made MGH my number one choice for anesthesia residency. In the following
decades Dick served as a devoted and fair leader, a thoughtful man who
delighted in growing his staff and developing their clinical and research skills.
Dick must surely hold the record for producing the most chairpersons of
anesthesia throughout the world.

Biographical note prepared by Warren M. Zapol, MD

■ Douglas M. Behrendt, MD

"You could be a good surgeon if you stopped watching yourself operate."

— to a surgical resident

A graduate of Amherst College and Harvard Medical School, Doug trained in general and cardiothoracic surgery at MGH, being the first (1971) to be chief resident in CT surgery as part of a newly constituted formal training program at MGH. A superb surgeon, he excelled as a teacher – some would say the best chief resident teacher we have seen in that position at MGH. He subsequently joined the CT surgical faculty at the University of Michigan after serving a fellowship in congenital heart surgery at Toronto's Hospital for Sick Children. Thereafter Doug was recruited to the University of Iowa as chief of Cardiothoracic Surgery. As the final chapter in a distinguished career emphasizing correction of (and resident training in the correction of) congenital heart defects in infants and children, Dr. Behrendt assumed the chair of the department of Surgery at Iowa.

Biographical note prepared by Willard M. Daggett, MD

■ Herman D. Suit, MD, DPhil

"I don't care where anyone is from just where they are going."

Herman Suit served as chair of Radiation Oncology for 30 years (1970–2000). He was thoroughly egalitarian. He did not care where anyone was from,

just where he or she was going. He always advised residents, fellows and staff to "look to the future." He advised his trainees and staff to judge each person as an individual with no consideration as to the tribal, linguistic, religious or geographic origin of that person. He encouraged people to realize that time is the most important asset that a human can have and is the only factor in life that is absolutely egalitarian. He urged people to accept the fact that each member of our species has no choice of even one gene, one parent, siblings and other relatives and the formative environment; to recognize that these genetic, cultural and environmental factors are the dominant determinants of the personality of the individual and of "success in life"; and to consider the unsuccessful as unlucky and that one's success is to a very large extent due to good luck.

Biographical note prepared by William U. Shipley, MD

■ Lloyd Axelrod, MD

To the residents and medical students on their first day on the
busiest internal medical service at the MGH:

**"We are engaged in the pursuit of
excellence as we understand it
without apology."**

This quote marked the first day of my first medical school clerkship and the
first day of my internship in internal medicine at the MGH, and set the tone
perfectly for two of the most intense months of patient care, teaching, and
learning that I have ever experienced. Dr. Axelrod introduced us to Team 1,
one of the busiest internal medicine services at the MGH, with this quote. It
encapsulates perfectly the goal of every MGH physician in the laboratory, the
teaching ward, or the clinic – to achieve excellence within the limits of our
understanding and to expand those limits to the greatest extent possible.

— *submitted by Michael E. Pacold, MD, PhD*

**"Follow-up is what separates the
amateurs from the pros in our profession.
It is the internalized 'running scared' that
keeps you on the cutting edge during a
long career in the practice of medicine."**

**"Medicine is a privileged window on
science and the human condition."**

These quotes capture the essence of philosophy and professionalism of
Lloyd Axelrod. His skills and knowledge as an experienced physician/educator
have served the MGH well during his 44 years at this hospital. During his
23 years as chief of the James Howard Means Firm, a major teaching arm of the
Department of Medicine, he steadfastly pursued and taught the human aspects
of medical care as well as clinical excellence. As an educator he pioneered the
adoption of interactive rather than passive teaching.

Lloyd has made numerous scholarly and investigative contributions in several areas, including the medical uses of glucocorticoids and the pathogenesis and treatment of diabetes and hypoglycemic syndromes. His interests have also extended to international health where, for example, he contributed in collaboration with the late Dr. George Hatem to the introduction of screening programs for neonatal hypothyroidism and phenylketonuria in China.

This remarkable range of achievements typifies Lloyd's commitment to excellence in all phases of medicine at this institution.

Biographical note prepared by John T. Potts, Jr., MD

■ Eve Elizabeth Slater, MD

"The richness of the experience derives from a rather
unique paradox and such paradox will represent
your greatest challenge. On the one hand to be
chief resident in Medicine at the MGH is to
have almost unlimited freedom. You are at liberty to
contribute a style and character to the Medical Services
that is inimitably your own ...

"What then constitutes the paradox?
As with all freedoms, there is inherent law.
Thus you are free, only so far as the needs of
the house staff, students and faculty will allow.
It is the privilege of the chief resident to be
the single person closest to problems and human failings.
Thus you must always be willing and able to be distracted
from the larger goal to provide
insight, emotional support, balance,
discipline, counsel and conciliation.

"... My own particular and personal goal was to provide an
example that women in medicine can function effectively in a
leadership capacity without sacrificing femininity."

— *from a letter to Gary K. Schoolnik, MD, Dr. Slater's successor as
chief resident in Medicine*

Eve Slater grew up in Spring Lake, NJ, and graduated from Vassar College and
the Columbia University College of Physicians and Surgeons. She completed
medical residency and a fellowship in cardiology at MGH. In 1976 she was
the first woman to be appointed chief resident in medicine in the history
of the hospital. From 1977 to 1982 she was chief of the Hypertension Unit,
studying hypertension and aortic diseases.

In 1983 Eve became senior director of Biochemical Endocrinology at Merck
Research Laboratories, leading teams of molecular biologists in the study of
receptors, endocrine disorders and atherosclerosis. Her own research focused on
signal transduction, publishing with Nobel laureates Robert J. Lefkowitz

and Brian K. Kobilka on the cloning of the mammalian beta-receptor. In 1990 she became leader of Merck's worldwide Regulatory Affairs group. She was promoted to vice president of Clinical and Regulatory Development in 1990 and senior vice president in 1994, the first woman to attain these positions. From 2007 to 2009 Eve was senior vice president, Worldwide Policy at Pfizer, Inc.

In 2001 Eve was nominated by President George W. Bush to be Assistant Secretary for Health, a position she held until 2003. In that position she oversaw the United States Public Health Service. During her tenure special emphasis was given to bioterrorism, the protection of human subjects, health care reform, women's health, the care of the elderly and HIV/AIDS. She received the Virginia Kneeland Frantz Distinguished Women in Medicine Award from P&S in 2003 and was featured in the NIH National Library of Medicine Exhibition "Changing the Face of Medicine: Celebrating America's Women Physicians."

Eve is also an accomplished flutist, having studied with several of America's foremost flutists. In 1975 she was asked by Arthur Fiedler, conductor of the Boston Pops Orchestra, to play with the orchestra at MGH Night at the Pops. She told Fiedler she could not be ready that year but would be able to do so the next year. Fiedler replied: "If I am alive next year I will invite you," to which Eve replied "This would be like playing for the Boston Red Sox." She played the Mozart Flute Concerto No. 2 with the Pops in 1976.

Eve is currently on the faculty of Columbia University College of Physicians and Surgeons, where she has taught in various positions since 1983.

Biographical note prepared by Lloyd Axelrod, MD

■ W. Scott McDougal, MD

When supervising teaching rounds Dr. McDougal made it very clear:

"If you know the material, I'll tip my cap to you and move to the next person. If you don't know the material, just say so. Don't fake it because I will know."

Dr. W. Scott McDougal was chief of Urology at the MGH from 1990 to 2012. During that time he dedicated his efforts to clinical care and research but especially to one on one teaching of the residents. He was known in the field as a dedicated teacher.

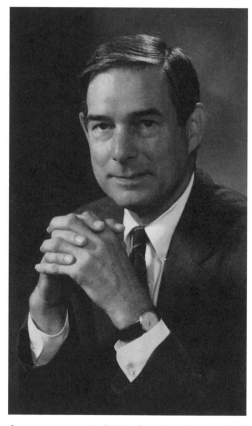

Dr. McDougal served on the National Board of Medical Examiners and the Examination Committee of the American Board of Urology. He served six years on the American Board of Urology and became its president. In 1996 he received the Russell and Mary Hugh Scott Award for Teaching and Education. And in 2011 he was honored with the Resident Teaching Award of the American Urological Association.

Every Tuesday morning at 6:30am he met with the Urology residents to go over a section of Campbell's *Textbook of Urology*. He had also done this with residents at the two programs he had previously chaired. He did the entire book in a three-year period. By the time he arrived at the MGH he had studied Campbell's Urology intensively for 10 years and while at the MGH he studied it for another 20 years. With good reason he was known to be encyclopedic. So, when he told the residents he would know if they didn't know the material he wasn't kidding.

Biographical note prepared by Stephen P. Dretler, MD

Alex F. Althausen, MD

"Approach every case with a script in mind, a plan, if you will."

So I knew which steps he wanted me to do, in what order and with which technique. Having a plan in mind for each case has served me well, and I have never become "lost" during urologic surgery. If, as a resident, I arrived at each step knowing the next move, I would be more of a participant in the operation.

— submitted by Raymond K. Whelan, MD

Alex Frederick Althausen was born in Riga, Latvia in 1940. His family made its way to the United States and Dr. Althausen graduated from Hofstra University and then Tufts Medical School. He did his first two years of surgical training at Albany Medical Center. He then served in Vietnam, had experience with battlefield surgery and was awarded the Bronze Star for his Army Medical Corps service.

After two years in the U.S. Army he came to the MGH, took an extra year of surgical training and subsequently completed the urology training program. In 1974 he joined the urology staff.

Over the years Dr. Althausen was lauded for his willingness and ability to take on difficult surgical problems and became the "go to" urologist for complicated oncologic urology. His work ethic was legendary, and he was known to make rounds seven days a week. He was committed to giving exemplary care, was loved by his patients and was highly respected by the urology and surgical residents. He was a teacher and mentor and was always available to give assistance. Because he took on such difficult problems, he had to plan his procedures meticulously and always had a "plan."

In 1988 Dr. Althausen was elected president of the New England Section of the American Urology Association. He won the Grayson Carroll Essay Award for Clinical Research sponsored by the American Urology Association.

Dr. Althausen retired at age 65 and at this writing is well and engaged in nonmedical activities.

Biographical note prepared by Stephen P. Dretler, MD

Francis J. McGovern, MD

"Even a prehistoric creature like a lobster uses both claws. If you are not using both hands in surgery you should know there is a problem."

Dr. Francis McGovern joined the staff at the MGH after completing his residency and chief residency in urology in 1989. Though he has practiced all aspects of urology throughout his career, he has focused on urologic oncology, treating thousands of patients with prostate, bladder, kidney, testis, and other genitourinary malignancies. Frank operates with an attention to detail that is second to none. The dissections and exposures are methodical, the steps are logical, the hemostasis is meticulous, and the goal of eliminating a potentially morbid or lethal cancer if at all possible is always accomplished. Many graduates of the MGH urology residency from the 1990s to the present credit Frank with teaching them about open surgery and specifically open surgery

of the pelvis. Former graduates (myself included) can hear his words as we enter the operating room to do a procedure in the pelvis – "set it up like a prostate." A former college standout swimmer and 2014 inductee into the Rhode Island Swimming Hall of Fame, Frank credits his athletic training for giving him the determination to be a methodical and successful surgeon.

There is another side to Frank that deserves mention – his kindness. He has an infectious smile and laugh that make a person feel comfortable. He is always available for consultation, be it from the surgical intern or the chief of the department. When I came to the MGH as a surgical intern, people often asked me which program I was from. When I answered "urology" their response was often, "Oh, you are so lucky to train here – Dr. McGovern is the nicest guy." His patients adore him for his compassion, and several whom I have seen after referral from him referred to him as a "saint." Frank's teaching and friendship have been invaluable to me during my time at MGH and are sure to be in the future.

Biographical note prepared by Brian H. Eisner, MD

■ Nina E. Tolkoff-Rubin, MD

"How are you, dear?"

"That's exactly right."

"Why should it be easy when it can be difficult?"

A characteristic story about Nina concerns the time she was a patient herself recovering from an intestinal operation on the 8th floor of the old Phillips House building. In the middle of the night early in her recovery, while she was still on intravenous support and with a nasogastric tube, she heard that one of her kidney transplant patients had suffered a cardiac arrest down the hall from her room. Without hesitation, she got herself up, made her way down the hall and supervised the patient's resuscitation.

Nina graduated with honors from Cornell University in 1964 and from Harvard Medical School in 1968, again with honors. Her postgraduate training in medicine

and nephrology was all at the MGH; she joined the medical staff in 1972. She was soon engaged in all aspects of the care of severely ill patients, assuming a guiding role in the hospital's first intensive care unit on Bulfinch 3. In 1974 she was made director of the Hemodialysis Unit and of the medical aspects of renal transplantation, as the two efforts were closely coordinated.

Nina has made many contributions to the care of patients with challenging problems ranging from complex metabolic derangements to difficult social and ethical issues. Often working closely with her talented husband, Robert, an expert in infectious diseases, she has recorded useful and well-conceived additions to the medical literature. Her contributions have been recognized by her promotion to a full professorship at HMS and by numerous other signs of recognition by colleagues near and far. The successful pursuit of her position calls for special gifts in bringing experts from different disciplines together to permit essential collaborations both in research and patient management. Her success, and the esteem she has earned in the halls of the MGH, are a consequence of her sterling personal qualities and the example she sets each day for those around her.

Biographical note prepared by Paul S. Russell, MD

Richard P. Cambria, MD

**"That was a tough case.
I couldn't have done it without you.
If it were any harder,
I couldn't have done it with you."**

Dr. Cambria has been a role model and mentor to many young vascular surgeons during his career. Nationally, he is known as a technically gifted surgeon with a quick wit on the podium and an encyclopedic knowledge of the literature. However, as a former trainee, it is the time spent with him in the operating room that is most memorable. He has a repertoire of pearls of wisdom and pithy comments that all of the fellows must absorb and digest as a rite of passage into the fraternity of central aortic surgeons. As I operate now, I hear his voice reminding me to "get on the aorta and stay on the aorta" or that operative success is "all in the set up." After one particularly long and arduous case, Dr. Cambria scrubbed out while I was closing. As he left the room he turned to me and said with a smile "that was a tough case pal. I couldn't have done it without you, and I almost couldn't do it *with* you." The experience of being the fellow on Dr. Cambria's service leaves an indelible impression on one as a surgeon and all of his trainees feel honored to have scrubbed across from him.

Biographical note prepared by Mark F. Conrad, MD, MMSc

■ Charles M. Ferguson, MD

Dr. Charlie Ferguson (a Georgia country boy) on the
three principles of surgery:

**"Cut well,
tie well,
git well."**

This often cited aphorism was sometimes used by Charles Ferguson, the
MGH Surgery residency director from 1998 until 2012, as a teaching point
for residents. He said that it was introduced to the lexicon of the teaching
service by Dr. E. Stanley Crawford, himself a former MGH resident in
surgery, during a Richardson Lectureship visit.

Charles, like his father, was a graduate of the residency program, and had a
central role in the education of many of his residents. He was a Georgia native,
but scarcely a "country boy," having grown up near Atlanta and graduated from
the Emory University School of Medicine. His use of "git" was part of his
exceptional skill in reproducing the linguistic nuances of the rural South.

Gifted as a general surgeon, he also excelled as a teacher and in his perception
of the idiosyncrasies of the department and staff, about which he was
sometimes outspoken.

Biographical note prepared by Leslie W. Ottinger, MD

Robert R. Linton, MD

"You have to do it right (my boy)."

As you know, Robert Linton was my hero and role model. I am sure that you remember his most famous quotation in response to how he achieved such good results in the early days of vascular surgery. He would predictably respond, "you have to do it right" (often adding for the residents' benefit, "my boy"). Linton recognized that vascular surgery was an unusually demanding specialty, with very little tolerance for errors in either judgment or technique. To obtain good results one must have a good understanding of vascular hemodynamics and physiology, as well as a good operative plan, at least one contingency alternative and, above all, meticulous execution in the operating room — in short, "you have to do it right."
— *submitted by Bruce S. Cutler, MD*

Robert Linton emigrated with his father from Scotland to Burton, Washington at the age of four. He graduated from the University of Washington, and then from Harvard Medical School in 1926. He spent two summers, during medical school, in the physiology laboratory of Walter B. Cannon working with an isolated heart preparation. This experience stimulated his interest in surgery, and two years later he started his surgical internship at the MGH. At that time, E.P. Richardson was the Homans Professor of Surgery. His goal was to develop a full-time teaching service. Richardson appointed Linton chief of the West Surgical Service in 1928. Richardson had come to regard Linton as his protégé, and his career at the MGH seemed assured. However, Richardson suffered a career-ending stroke in 1930 and his successor, Edward Churchill, believed that Linton was headed for a clinical career that did not fit with his plans for a full-time, research-oriented teaching service. Churchill eventually appointed Linton to the surgical staff as a pediatric surgeon (a non-existent specialty at the time).

Competition for cases was intense among young surgeons at the MGH, so Linton looked for opportunities to establish his reputation in areas not of interest to others. He began by refining and perfecting the treatment of varicose veins and the post phlebitis syndrome. He went on to develop the Linton balloon for the tamponade of bleeding esophageal varices, and popularized the spleno-renal shunt for the treatment of portal hypertension. He was the first at the MGH to implant aortic homografts, and also the first to abandon their use in favor of nylon and later Dacron prosthetic grafts. A year after Kunlin implanted a saphenous vein graft in France, Linton performed the first venous interposition graft for a popliteal aneurysm. More than any other, the saphenous vein femoropopliteal graft became Linton's operation because of its durability and the technical expertise required for good outcomes.

December 8, 1970 may have been Linton's finest day. He resected a suprarenal aortic aneurysm and replaced it with a Dacron graft extending from the diaphragm to the femoral arteries, with side arms for the celiac, mesenteric and renal vessels. Although such a procedure would not be considered unusual by modern standards, it was a tour de force at that time. After the case was presented at Surgical Grand Rounds one of his colleagues commented, "At the conclusion of the presentation, something happened that was unique and unprecedented. The audience, including the usually reserved and chary surgeons, arose and applauded. Bob Linton was more than 70 years old."

Linton's career of more than 40 years at the MGH spanned the full evolution of reconstructive vascular surgery and laid the groundwork for further developments in open and endovascular procedures. Of equal importance was his observation that vascular surgery was an unusually demanding specialty with very limited tolerance for errors in either judgment or technique. He admonished a generation of aspiring vascular surgeons by his remark, "more than anything else, to achieve good results, you must do it right."

Biographical note prepared by Bruce S. Cutler, MD

Bruce S. Cutler, MD

"In vascular surgery nothing is impossible."

"The smaller the indication for operation the bigger the complication."

"One complication often begets another."

"Good results in vascular surgery require that you do the right operation, at the right time, and do it right."

Ever a stickler for precision in language, Bruce Cutler is precise and thorough in everything he does: presentations, furniture making, writing and editing manuscripts, patient care and, of course, operations.

After graduating with honors from Princeton University and Harvard Medical School, Cutler became an MGH surgical intern in 1966. He served in Vietnam (Colin Powell was his commanding officer) before resuming his MGH residency and then extending it with a vascular surgery fellowship under Jesse Thompson.

He was one of the founding surgeons of the University of Massachusetts Medical School, where he spent his entire career. He rapidly progressed to professor, chief of Vascular Surgery and director of the Vascular Surgery Fellowship program.

Bruce was one of the best surgeons I ever knew. Precision, persistence, superb anatomic and physiologic knowledge, originality and inventiveness, and technical skill marked his every operation. Never did any surgeon take more conscientious care of his patients. Never was there a surgeon more demanding of his residents. Just ask them. But, as they would also agree, never was there a better, more dedicated teacher, and his demands of his residents were exceeded many times over by his demands of himself.

Linton was his hero; he outdid Linton.

Biographical note prepared by Thomas J. Vander Salm, MD

THE 9PM MEAL

by Alice Chen-Plotkin, MD

We would be working like crazy somewhere or other during on-call nights, and then there would be this must-not-miss hour where the free 9pm meal would be served. As the senior resident, I'd page all the juniors and the medical students to remind them to go down to the basement cafeteria to eat – usually something that was similar to a bad Thanksgiving-day meal (turkey, cranberry sauce, mashed potatoes, questionable salad, Pepsi if the fountain machine was working – 50/50 chance). You'd see all the other on-call residents down there, and the cafeteria would be full of humor (sometimes toxically tinged) and a spirit of camaraderie. We would sometimes cheer when the last member of the team on call arrived from wherever they had been working in the hospital, and everyone had made it to the 9pm meal.

STRONG WORK

Lauren Glickman, MD, recalls from her residency the expression "strong work," which is what supervising medical residents would say to medical interns when they took unusually good care of a patient, made an astute observation, prevented a catastrophe or had all lab values and x-rays in order.

IT'S NOT THE SUTURE

"Soon after I arrived, I was scrubbing with Dr. Marshall Bartlett. After breaking two or three sutures, I looked disgustedly at the broken tie and Jenny, Dr. Bartlett's long time scrub nurse, said, 'It's not the suture, it's just the jerk on the end of the knot.' This relieved the tension and I became a good assistant."

— *Anonymous*

■ Raymond D. Adams, MD

Dr. Adams, who was not a fan of long lists for
differential diagnosis, used to say to
residents and students something like this:

"Please don't tell me all the wrong diagnoses,
tell me the correct one ..."

Raymond Delacy Adams became chair of the Department of Neurology
at MGH in 1951 and, as the Bullard Professor of Neuropathology, Harvard
Medical School, directed the department until 1978. His quarter century
tenure spanned an epoch in which methods of investigation and models of
disease that had held sway for much of a century were challenged radically
by a virtual renaissance of neuroscience, embodied in the Neuroscience
Study Program, which coalesced in the environment of the MGH. It was an
epoch that readied the clinical neurosciences for the coming explosions of
conceptual and methodological vistas, extending from the development of
computerized imaging to the discovery of restriction endonucleases and the
opening of the eukaryotic genome.

Raymond Adams was among the structural columns of this ferment. He
was fundamentally a scientist, critical, challenging, and objective. He was the
uncontested master of inquiry and analysis within the scope of the gross
and microscopic histopathology of the nervous and muscular systems and of
correlations with the disorders he encountered in the clinic. An extensive primary
bibliography and, importantly, his texts published variously in monograph
form with colleagues Fisher, Richardson, Victor and others as coauthors set the
contemporary standard of clinical-pathological science and exposition, relating to
discoveries in virtually every domain of human neurological disease and disability.
The repeatedly updated chapters on the nervous system in Harrison's *Principles of
Internal Medicine* document a critical maturation of the methods and precision of
anatomic description and clinical-pathological correlation that carried forward in
the decades that followed.

With colleagues Philip Dodge, Hugo Moser and others, the department of
Neurology formalized a division of Child Neurology and extended its scope
of investigations, clinical care and training to the WE Fernald State School,
sponsoring the establishment of the Shriver Center and activation of the

Southard Laboratory of Developmental Pathology on its premises. This outreach focused on fundamental investigations into the normal and disordered development of the nervous system.

Raymond Adams was an educator with influence achieved with fellows, residents and students that carried forward as a standard in human brain science. The clinical or clinical pathology training experienced was intensive – at the bedside, in the clinic, or in the pathology laboratory. The graduates of the program under his direction in the years that followed were among the leaders of major programs both in this country and abroad.

Raymond Adams was above all a physician deeply sensitive to the complexity of the human condition and its disabilities. Among the reflections of this that he has left with us was the reminder:

"If you lose your temper with a patient, you have forfeited your privilege to serve as that patient's physician."

Biographical note prepared by Verne S. Caviness, Jr., MD

CMF

By Robert H. Ackerman, MD

C. Miller Fisher (CMF), emeritus professor of Neurology, who died on April 14, 2012, was a principal founder of modern stroke neurology. Amongst his many contributions to the field were his findings that extra-cranial carotid artery disease and atrial fibrillation were frequent causes of ischemic stroke. The discovery of these two potentially preventable sources of ischemic events swept away long-standing theories of vasospasm and of middle cerebral artery thrombosis as the primary causes of cerebral ischemia, opening a new era of stroke diagnosis and management.

CMF's memorable bedside teaching often was punctuated by adage and by example. Illustrative of the former, he frequently reminded residents and fellows,

"The care of the patient is the most important thing,"

and, indicative of the latter, Dr. Fisher was the bedside model of patience and observation, as witnessed, for example, by Dr. Edward Wolpow during morning rounds in the 1960s. As the neurology team arrived at the bedside of a semi-comatose patient with known severe bilateral medial-frontal brain damage due to a ruptured anterior cerebral artery aneurysm, Dr. Fisher issued a lively, "Good morning." The patient did not answer. CMF, suspecting an abulic syndrome (delayed cognitive/motor responsiveness), said he would wait for a reply. Twenty-six minutes later the patient returned the greeting. Dr. Fisher was there to receive it.

■ Benjamin Castleman, MD

**"Special stains give you an extra day to
think about the diagnosis."**

"Remember there is a patient at the other end of the slide."

Benjamin Castleman, chief of Pathology at MGH from 1953–1974 and a
professor of Pathology at Harvard Medical School, was famous for his editorship
and promotion of the Case Records of the MGH published weekly in the
New England Journal of Medicine, as well as his pioneering contributions to the

pathology of the parathyroid glands, heart, lungs,
lymph nodes and other organs. He was beloved
as a teacher by his residents, with whom he
typically spent two hours a day teaching the
basic and fine points of pathology and imparting
his wisdom and judgment on clinical matters.

He came to the MGH as a pathology intern
after graduating from Yale Medical School.
During his residency he began his pioneering
autopsy study of the anatomy of the parathyroid
glands with Dr. Oliver Cope, then a surgical
resident. In 1935 he joined the MGH staff as an assistant pathologist, rising to the
rank of professor of Pathology and chief of Pathology in 1953.

Among the subjects of his memorable publications were a newly recognized
lymph node disorder that led to the eponym "Castleman's disease," the
pathology and radiology of pulmonary emboli (with Dr. Aubrey O. Hampton),
the first systematic renal biopsy study of hypertension (with Dr. Reginald H.
Smithwick), the high incidence of atheromatous emboli to the kidney after
aortic surgery (that led to improved surgical techniques), and the pathology and
dynamics of rheumatic and calcific aortic valve disease. His name is perpetuated
in the hospital he loved by the bestowal on his successors as chiefs of Pathology
the title "The Benjamin Castleman Professor of Pathology," which was activated
two weeks before his death on June 29, 1982.

*Biographical note excerpted and edited by Robert B. Colvin, MD, from "Benjamin
Castleman" by Robert E. Scully, MD, in Keen Minds to Explore the Dark
Continents of Disease, Louis DN and Young RH, eds, 2011*

Austin L. Vickery, Jr., MD

"When you are examining a slide with your microscope at high power and you are thinking about diagnosing parathyroid carcinoma, lie down until the urge goes away."

— regarding pathological diagnosis of a rare tumor

Austin Lorenzo Vickery, Jr., MD (Vic), a professor of Pathology at MGH, was an international leader in the pathology of thyroid diseases and made many contributions in the fields of gastrointestinal and prostate diseases. Born in Omaha, Nebraska on August 18, 1919, he graduated from the University of Nebraska Medical School with honors in 1943. Originally seeking a career in surgery, he trained at the Peter Bent Brigham Hospital and later the Cleveland Clinic, but had to abandon his goal due to a wrist injury that limited his manual dexterity. He was recruited by Dr. Tracy B. Mallory as an assistant pathologist in January 1949. That month marked the beginning of a half-century of service to the MGH that was interrupted only by a two-year leave of absence to serve in Tokyo as a captain in the U.S. Army during the Korean conflict, along with his close friend and colleague, Dr. Robert E. Scully. The most memorable papers of Dr. Vickery regarding the thyroid gland addressed the pathology and treatment of well-differentiated thyroid papillary carcinoma, the effects of radioactive iodine on the thyroid and the value of the needle biopsy for diagnosis and follow-up.

Dr. Vickery was an imposing figure, tall and athletic-appearing, towering above most of the laboratory personnel. He was almost always cautious and deliberate in making important decisions in his personal life and in the laboratory. He would sometimes rise from his chair at the microscope and pace in his office before giving an answer to a controversial proposal. Some young residents were terrified on entering his office for fear of receiving a scolding, but he was greatly admired and respected. His wit was legendary. He was famous for his aphorisms.

Dr. Vickery retired from the active MGH staff in 1998. In June, 2000, he and his wife Frances endowed the Austin L. Vickery, Jr. Harvard Medical School Professorship in Pathology at the MGH, whose first incumbent is Dr. Nancy L. Harris, a world-renowned hemato-pathologist. They later left a substantial endowment to the MGH to be used at the discretion of Dr. Robert Colvin, then the chief of the department. Dr. Vickery said that the money was what his Danish grandmother called "cash money." Among other things the funds are currently used for "Vickery grants" to help defray costs associated with residents' research projects. Dr. Vickery died on March 2, 2005. His wit, wisdom and philanthropy remain his legacy, in addition to his solid contributions to pathology and medicine.

Biographical note excerpted and edited by Robert B. Colvin, MD, from "Austin L. Vickery, Jr." by Robert E. Scully, MD, in Keen Minds to Explore the Dark Continents of Disease, Louis DN and Young RH, eds, 2011

WHAT WOULD YOU CALL IT?

Austin L. Vickery, Jr., MD, and Robert E. Scully, MD, long-time surgical pathologists and friends at MGH:

Scully, while showing a case to Vickery:
"Vic, if you were taking the board exams and saw this case, what would you call it?"

Vickery:
"Well, I'd call it a malignant tumor and most likely of gynecological origin."

Scully:
"And, Vic, what would you call it when you were taking the board exams for the second time?"

REINVENTION

Gordon (Butch) Donaldson, MD, commenting
on a current clinical paper:

**"Things need to be re-invented
every ten years."**

■ Robert E. Scully, MD

"That is a very good diagnosis, but why don't we sign the case out using my opinion."

The quoted remark made by Dr. Robert E. Scully to a trainee is only one of many examples of the gentle character of a stalwart member of the department of Pathology at the MGH for 54 years. A native of Massachusetts and 1944 graduate of Harvard Medical School, Dr. Scully trained at the Peter Bent Brigham Hospital, but spent his entire postgraduate career at the MGH with the exception of two years in the armed services during the Korean conflict. He was a legendary diagnostic pathologist with remarkable skills at the microscope but also a person with great knowledge of medicine and surgery, which served him well when he was the editor of the *Case Records of the Massachusetts General Hospital,* published in the *New England Journal of Medicine,* for a remarkable and record span of 27 years. His broad knowledge also served well many patients because, particularly in the circumstance of unusual tumors upon which Dr. Scully consulted, it was often his advice that led to the appropriate management. Although knowledgeable on essentially all areas of pathology, Dr. Scully took a special interest in gynecological pathology and testicular pathology and became internationally recognized for his work in those areas. He is largely responsible for the current pathologic classification of female genital tract tumors and described many new entities. He was the founding president of the International Society of Gynecological Pathologists and received countless awards throughout his distinguished career.

After his retirement, Dr. Scully continued to consult as needed from his home and remained in close contact with many members of the department of Pathology and numerous friends from far and wide all of whom held him in great affection. An annual prize for a young investigator is offered in Dr. Scully's name at the annual meeting of the International Society of Gynecological Pathologists and an annual lectureship in his name is held by the New England Society of Pathologists. Near the end of his life donations from his many devoted trainees and former colleagues resulted in the endowment of the Robert E. Scully Professorship of Pathology at Harvard Medical School.

Biographical note prepared by Robert H. Young, MD

RESEARCH

Fuller Albright, MD

**"Science emerged from metaphysics when
people began to make measurements."**

The next four quotations come from Albright's presidential address to the
American Society of Clinical Investigation in 1941, with a wonderful figure
on "Dos and Do Nots" along the road leading to the Castle of Success in
Clinical Investigation.

"Look from all sides."
"Measure something."
"[Do not be a] lone wolf."

**"See to it that you do not wake up some fine morning in an
executive job. Do not show too much administrative ability.
The first time you are asked to serve on a committee, be
anything but efficient. Never make the mistake of proposing
some new reform; you are apt to be chosen as a committee of
one to put said reform through. Whatever else you do, do not
become a professor of Medicine or the head of a department."**

**"My interests have not been limited to any one field by grants
of money or other barriers. As a result, my studies have
flitted from this to that and back to this again."**

On one occasion, one of his associates addressed an Ether Dome assemblage
at the MGH and discussed parathyroid disease in rather dogmatic fashion.
Afterward, Albright was asked to comment. He replied:

"I would only like to add a few ifs, buts and maybes."

Alexander Leaf, MD, made the next two observations:

"I saw Fuller angry only once – about an attempt to keep research secret."

"Dr. Fuller Albright could extract more meaning from a blackboard of
data than anyone else I ever knew," describing Albright's delineation of
adrenal hormones.

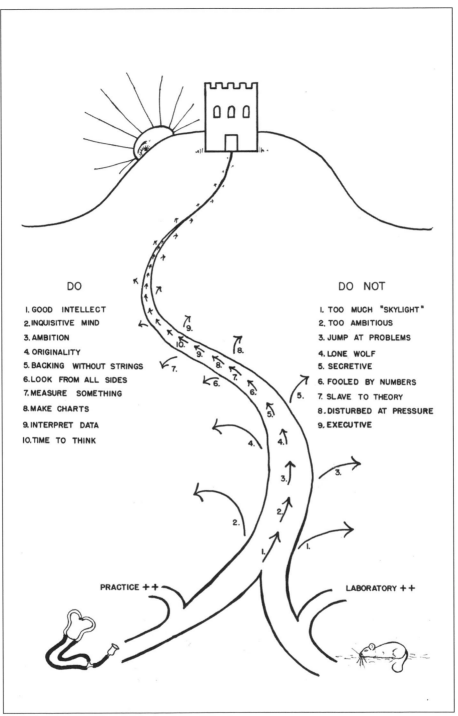

Some of Dr. Albright's "Dos and Do Nots"

Albright F., *Journal of Clinical Investigation* 1944; 23:921-926

Anne P. Forbes, MD, noted, describing Albright's definition of pseudohypoparathyroidism: "Fuller saw things others missed."

Fuller Albright, the father of modern endocrinology, was the first chief of the Endocrine Unit at the MGH. An institution at Harvard Medical School and the MGH during his career, he became a legendary figure after his professional efforts were terminated by the relentless progression of Parkinson's disease and the tragic consequences of surgical intervention. Albright contributed in major ways to our understanding of calcium metabolism, the function and disorders of the parathyroid glands, metabolic bone disease, kidney stones, inherited endocrine disorders, and diseases of the adrenal glands, ovaries, testes and pituitary gland.

The legend of Fuller Albright is compounded of the description of numerous syndromes and the elucidation of many mechanisms of disease, of defiance of a disabling illness and of puckish humor. Of his disease he wrote:

"For the past 10 years I have had the interesting experience of observing the development of Parkinson's syndrome on myself. As a matter of fact, the condition does not come under my special medical interests, or else I am sure I would have had it solved long ago."

Biographical note prepared by Lloyd Axelrod, MD

■ Anne P. Forbes, MD

"Of course you can describe a new syndrome. Just go into the clinic and look for a patient whose findings do not fit into a conventional category."

At least one endocrine fellow heeded this advice and described a new syndrome.

Nan Forbes began her endocrine fellowship with Dr. Fuller Albright at the MGH in 1939, and then spent her career in the Endocrine Unit of the hospital as a colleague and collaborator. She was an outstanding clinician, educator and investigator. With Dr. Albright she described the syndrome of amenorrhea (loss of menstrual periods), galactorrhea (milk flow in women who are not pregnant) and a pituitary tumor years before the hormone prolactin was discovered. For many years the syndrome was known as the Forbes-Albright syndrome. After the identification of prolactin and the recognition that some pituitary tumors are associated with excessive secretion of this hormone, the entity became known as the prolactinoma syndrome. Forbes played an important role in the establishment of the Ovarian Dysfunction Clinic at the MGH. Early in her career she became one of the first female members of the American Society for Clinical Investigation.

Nan was an early advocate of family planning. In a letter to the editor of the *New England Journal of Medicine* published on December 27, 1973, she wrote in part,

"Why should not every doctor, regardless of his area of special interest, make a practice of asking all patients if they have adequate contraceptive care? ... To offer advice or referral to such patients is the least we can do."

As noted in her obituary in the *Boston Globe* in 1992, "In retirement, Dr. Forbes took up farming, keeping a large garden, some ponies and a flock of sheep that she sheared herself. She would spin and dye the wool by hand and she liked to demonstrate these arts in the Milton schools."

Biographical note prepared by Lloyd Axelrod, MD

Alexander Leaf, MD

**"Medicine is a service profession.
There are many ways to serve.
You will serve best if you do
what you love most."**

**"Academic researchers need to
investigate disease mechanisms.
If we don't, nobody will."**

Alexander Leaf was chief of the Department of Medicine at MGH and Jackson Professor of Medicine at Harvard Medical School from 1966 to 1981.

Alex was born in Yokohama, Japan in 1920 to parents who fled Russia after the Bolshevik revolution. The family moved to Seattle in 1922. He received a BS in Chemistry at the University of Washington and an MD from the University of Michigan in 1943. He came in 1944 as an intern in Medicine to MGH, was a resident at the Mayo Clinic and fellow at the University of Michigan and then returned in 1949 to MGH, working first with Fuller Albright and then setting up his own small lab. In 1954 he spent four months in Copenhagen with biophysicist Hans Ussing, and was introduced to the toad bladder as a model for membrane transport. He then spent two years at Oxford with biochemist Hans Krebs.

Returning to MGH as chief of the Cardiorenal Laboratories, he continued groundbreaking studies that illuminated the mechanisms of transport across cell membranes and control of water balance in the body, fundamental to understanding renal physiology.

Although his clear physiological thinking made him an outstanding teacher in small groups, his shy, quiet speech and slight stammer were not as successful in the lecture hall.

Always interested in the contributions of diet and exercise to health, he studied centenarians in the mountains of Peru, the Hunza Valley of Pakistan and the Caucasus. He was a jogger and stair-climber before those activities were widespread.

He promoted the primary care residency program at MGH, and was a founding member of Physicians for Social Responsibility in 1961, opposing nuclear proliferation. As Ridley Watts Professor, he chaired the HMS Department of Preventive Medicine and Clinical Epidemiology from 1980 to 1990.

After formal retirement, he continued in his laboratory studying the effects of fish oil and fatty acids in reducing ventricular arrhythmias. He died in December 2012 at age 92.

Biographical note prepared by Cecil H. Coggins, MD

■ Judah M. Folkman, MD

"As long as there is an unconquered disease, an injury that cannot be repaired or a method of prevention that remains beyond our reach, we have an obligation to conduct research."

"Research represents HOPE, and for many patients and families HOPE is the best we have to offer. We pursue our investigations so that one day we can offer HEALTH."

Judah Folkman is recognized worldwide, primarily for his dogged pursuit of a cure for cancer using tumor-starving drugs. Yet, those of us who trained and worked with Judah most remember his selfless generosity with his time and his belief that nothing is impossible. I was an intern in 1965, during

Judah's year as chief surgical resident, when one of our patients developed acute renal failure requiring hemodialysis that wasn't then available at the MGH. Knowing that I had had experience with hemodialysis, Judah simply concluded that we would start our own program, which we did after building, from scratch, a dialysis machine from a discarded washing machine.

After completing his MGH surgical training, Judah at the age of 34 became the youngest ever professor and chair of Surgery at Children's Hospital Medical Center. It was at this point that he first theorized that blocking blood vessel growth into growing tumors would starve the cells to death. His theory of angiogenesis occupied the rest of his professional life, during which he often commented that

"there's a fine line between persistence and obstinacy."

When a number of anti-angiogenic drugs finally came to clinical trial, many concluded that Judah would soon receive the Nobel Prize for their discovery. Unfortunately, this became impossible when Judah at the age of 74 succumbed to a heart attack while traveling to deliver another of his many unforgettable lectures.

Biographical note prepared by A. Benedict Cosimi, MD

■ John T. Potts, Jr., MD

"It's only the people that count at this institution."

This quotation, heard frequently by his colleagues, typifies the leadership philosophy that has guided John Potts in his various leadership roles. He would often add that, of course, caring about the people is the secret of having the institution fulfill its missions.

John Potts graduated from La Salle College and the University of Pennsylvania Medical School before coming to the MGH for internal medicine training. He then spent eight years at NIH learning protein chemistry and, with his

collaborator Gerry Aurbach, isolating and then sequencing parathyroid hormone, thus beginning a continuing 50+ year career at the forefront of what is now called translational research. He became chief of the Endocrine Unit on his return to MGH in 1968 and then chief of Medicine in 1981. His tenure as chief until 1996 was characterized by explosive growth of the Medical Service and a consolidation of the Department of Medicine at the MGH as a pioneer in medical research. Dr. Potts was instrumental in the decisions to expand MGH research to Charlestown, to establish the department of Molecular Biology, and to build a modern cancer program at the MGH. He is particularly proud of his role in establishing a departmental Minority Recruitment Committee, whose success led to the establishment of the MGH Office of Minority Affairs, as well as the departmental Society of Research Fellows that he used to help guide the careers of many of the current leaders at the MGH. These roles exemplify his commitment to the mentoring of those at the MGH and around the world in academic medicine and beyond.

After stepping down as chair, Dr. Potts served as director of Research at the MGH for many years and today remains active in helping with a number of initiatives at the interface of MGH medicine and the biotech world. Dr. Potts is Principal Investigator of an NIH program project that has been renewed many times, now in its 46th year of funding.

Biographical note prepared by Henry M. Kronenberg, MD

■ Patricia K. Donahoe, MD

"It was a warm moment that I shall never forget ..."

"Early years at MGH in the late 60s and 70s were incredibly formative but also formidable, particularly if one were a 'girl' in surgery and had trained outside the MGH. Once one's resolve was recognized, however, support eventually became strong and sustained. I recall as I nervously rose to give my first paper at the American Surgical Association that all the senior stalwarts of the MGH Surgical Department returned to the auditorium to 'wave the flag.' It was a warm moment that I shall never forget, a tradition that my colleagues and I carried forward, and an inspiration for me throughout the next 40 years.

"Hours were long, but the learning curve was steep, particularly for W. Hardy Hendren's fellow or resident. The work was done willingly and with dedication, as we appreciated the opportunity to learn from the 'surgical masters' of the MGH. Camaraderie was high and moments between exhaustion and near disaster were filled with laughter and the excitement of making a difference. The 'masters' were raconteurs, always with a story, a joke, a moral aphorism, or a captured 'teaching moment,' not to be denied. Who cannot remember Dr. Hendren's head peeking into an operating room asking, 'How's the junior varsity doing?' Although the bar was set high, and despite the hours, families were foremost and the hours spent with them were doubly precious. We were mentored, looked after in ways that we never even knew, and protected when we strayed out of line. Forty years at the MGH where excellence and innovation are the mantra has been fun, satisfying, and rewarding, and colleagues have become lifelong friends because of mutual respect and pride in what we do collectively."

— *submitted by Patricia K. Donahoe, MD*

One summer day, Pat Donahoe arrived in front of our Cape Cod house armed with a brand new windsail. Clearly, this was the day Pat had decided she would master this new life experience. It soon became clear that on this windy day a major contest was going on right in front of me. I recall thinking: "Pat Donahoe vs. Mother Nature: Mother Nature doesn't stand a chance." Sure enough, Pat's wonderful "can do" confidence and dogged persistence won the day. An hour into a series of futile attempts that would have discouraged Job himself, Pat was soaring across the bay at an exhilarating rate of speed – only to realize that she had no idea of how to turn the contraption around. So she collapsed the sail and proceeded to teach herself how to initiate a deep-water start; she ultimately crashed her sailboard on the beach. Clearly, stopping was a nicety that was going to be a lesson for another day. This anecdote reveals all of Pat's wonderful attributes. She undertakes challenges others find too daunting and does so without complaint. She refuses to be intimidated by any obstacles and has a ferocious dedication to acquiring whatever skills are necessary to succeed. Ultimately, she charts pioneering courses on her own terms.

As a student in embryology, Pat learned that Mullerian Inhibiting Substance (MIS) is an endocrine/paracrine factor secreted from the gonads that causes regression of the female accessory reproductive system during male development when it is not needed. Reasoning that most ovarian cancers are Mullerian in origin, she developed the notion that MIS might well be useful to treat malignancies of Mullerian origin. Over the ensuing 40 years, Pat developed the sensitive biological assay systems required to monitor its purification and characterization. She cloned the MIS gene and expressed sufficient MIS protein to conduct the necessary experiments to test her idea. Assays for MIS (also known as anti–Mullerian hormone) are used in the evaluation of disorders of sexual differentiation, in the evaluation and management of infertility in women and to monitor tumors of Mullerian origin. MIS may someday be used to treat tumors of Mullerian origin.

She was the first woman professor of surgery in Harvard Medical School's history. She received the highest scientific award of the Endocrine Society, the Fred Conrad Koch Award, and was also one of the rare recipients of the MGH's Trustees Medal. She is a member of the Institute of Medicine and the National Academy of Sciences.

However, it is her remarkable patient care, her training of many generations of surgical house officers, her mentoring of several postdoctoral fellows and medical students, and her serving as a beacon for so many women physicians and scientists at the MGH and HMS that will be her enduring and intergenerational contributions.

Biographical note prepared by William F. Crowley, Jr., MD

■ P. Roy Vagelos, MD

"My experience at the MGH with critically ill patients on respirators during the last polio epidemic in Boston and the impact the next year of a vaccine that prevented this dread disease were the basis for my passion for disease prevention."

P. Roy Vagelos was for years the most admired CEO in the pharmaceutical industry, leading Merck to scientific eminence in the development of statins and the development of 5-alpha reductase inhibitors (used to treat enlargement of the prostate and male pattern baldness) while simultaneously donating treatment for river blindness in Africa and the technology for developing hepatitis B vaccine in China.

Roy grew up in New Jersey, the son of immigrant Greek parents. He attended the University of Pennsylvania, majoring in chemistry. (He subsequently was the chair of the Board of the University of Pennsylvania.) He then attended Columbia College of Physicians and Surgeons before coming to the MGH as an intern and resident. After a period at the NIH, followed by a leadership role in the department of Biochemistry at Washington University in St. Louis, he moved on to head Merck Research and ultimately the company.

Biographical note prepared by Samuel O. Thier, MD

MGH VALUES

"IT'S A BEAUTIFUL DAY."

by Michael E. Pacold, MD, PhD

It was a horrible day at the end of our surgical clerkship. Days were getting shorter and colder. The weather was foul and all of us were exhausted and miserable. At the beginning of the didactic session, Dr. Charles J. McCabe asked one of the students, "What kind of a day is it?" The student's reply: "It's a horrible day." Dr. McCabe would reply, "No, it's a beautiful day." Then he told us this story: He worked his way through college, medical school, a tough surgical residency and cardiothoracic fellowship at the MGH — and within a few years was stripped of his ability to operate and even to walk by MS. He told us how he had lived many miserable days and how he had found his calling in the Emergency Department and in teaching medical students. His wife, family and colleagues had supported him through this and now, every day was a beautiful day.

■ Edward D. Churchill, MD

"The medical profession with its commitment to change is a learning as well as a learned profession."

Edward Delos Churchill was born in Chenoa, Illinois. He attended Northwestern University, where he spent an extra year to earn a masters degree in biology, and then was given admission to Harvard Medical School as a second year student. His surgery training followed at the MGH. His unusual promise was early recognized and in 1931, at age 35, he was appointed the John Homans Professor of Surgery at Harvard and chief of the West Surgical Service, the academic service, at the MGH.

His achievements during his 30-year career here were notable. He made important contributions to clinical surgery, especially to that of the lungs and heart, to endocrine surgery, to burn care, and, during WW II, to military medicine. He developed a world-renowned Department of Surgery and a plan and philosophy of resident education that was widely emulated.

But more than this, he was a wise spokesman for balance and humanism in medicine and a treasured mentor and friend to two generations of MGH surgery residents.

Biographical note prepared by Leslie W. Ottinger, MD

■ Rita M. Kelley, MD

At the time of her death in 1981 her colleagues wrote:

"The care of the patient was Rita Kelley's lifelong concern: a careful diagnostic evaluation; the best available therapy; and, throughout the process, devotion to her patients – who reciprocated with total loyalty. There lay her interest and there her reward."

Her colleague, Howard Ulfelder, MD, said of her:

"The satisfaction she derived from treating people for relatively minor problems during busy working days gave balance to her life. She seemed to be everybody's first choice for a consultant."

Rita Marie Kelley graduated from Boston State Teachers College in 1938, but her plans to teach quickly became derailed. Shortly after graduation, her work as a research assistant in Dr. Ira Nathanson's lab at the Harvard Medical School facility for cancer patients, Huntington Memorial Hospital, came to the attention of chief of the Medical Department Joseph Aub. Convinced of her potential, he persuaded her to become a physician. After a year at the Massachusetts Institute of Technology, where she earned an MPH degree, Kelley attended the Columbia University College of Physicians and Surgeons. After she received her MD in 1946, Kelley  returned to Boston and began her 35-year career at the MGH, first as an intern, then as a research fellow in the Huntington Laboratories, by then incorporated into the MGH, and eventually becoming acting chief of Oncology, 1973–1976, and a clinical professor of Medicine at the Harvard Medical School in 1980.

Kelley became an internationally known cancer specialist, co-authoring pioneering papers on the use of chemotherapy in treating breast cancer and the use of hormones to treat endometrial and other cancers. At the time of her death in 1981, she was remembered particularly for her clinical skills, her compassion and her dedication to her patients.

Biographical note from the archives of the Francis A. Countway Library of Medicine, Harvard Medical School

■ Oliver Cope, MD

Oliver Cope, MD, was a professor of surgery at Harvard and a noted clinician at the MGH. He made innovations in the treatment of parathyroid disease and burns. He lived to be 92 and was active until his last years.

Late in his career he was seen by a former resident to be striding purposefully down a long corridor in the Wang Ambulatory Care Center.
He was approached by the former resident and greeted with "How are you Dr. Cope?" Dr. Cope stopped, fixed his steely blue-eyed gaze on the now young staff surgeon, and said,

"Young man, I haven't taken the time to look"
and resumed his rapid pace down the corridor.

During his long surgical career at the MGH, Cope combined scientific observation with compassion and concern for the emotional state of his patients. The Nazi persecution he witnessed during a travelling fellowship in Berlin made an impression that lasted his lifetime.

He contributed to the birth and development of parathyroid and thyroid surgery, the understanding and treatment of burn injury both before and after the catastrophic Cocoanut Grove fire in 1942, and the revolutionary acceptance of breast-conservation and other non-radical treatments of cancer. His Presidential Address to the American Surgical Association in 1963 called attention to the social dimension of surgical care and the emotional and psychological aspects of illness. His innovative views on medical education became embodied in Harvard Medical School's "New Pathway."

"The iconoclastic approach of Oliver Cope to medical orthodoxy, surgical operations, the education of students and residents, and curricular reform was that of a gentleman with strongly held and voiced convictions leavened with good humor and an abiding interest in the welfare of his students, his patients, and their families." *(Harvard Gazette,* 1997)

Biographical note prepared by Andrew L. Warshaw, MD

■ Grant V. Rodkey, MD

"There are no dull patients, only dull doctors."

"There is no such thing as an uninteresting patient."

"Your job at the MGH is to carry the ball for 15 yards and then to pass it on."

"At the MGH it is possible to pursue excellence and to pursue our dreams of social justice and never to feel that the two are in conflict."

Grant V. Rodkey was a member of the Allen team, assembled by Arthur W. Allen, the legendary chief of the East Surgical Service at the MGH. This team included Claude Welch, Gordon Donaldson, and Glen Behringer. Although

associated with these strong surgical personalities, Grant was able to maintain his own identity, and become a productive surgeon who toiled for decades at our hospital.

Clinically, Grant was unfailingly devoted to the best interests of his patients. His strongest personality trait was his unbounded sense of optimism, which washed over those around him. This has served him well throughout his long and productive life.

The capstone of his surgical career was his selection to receive the Nathan Smith Award, bestowed by the New England Surgical Society. This is the highest honor that can be conferred on a member for his or her life's work in the field of surgery.

Biographical note prepared by Ashby C. Moncure, MD

■ Martin C. Mihm, MD

"Working at the MGH is not a job, it is a way of life."

Dr. Martin C. Mihm, Jr. started his 50-year association with the MGH in 1964. He was one of the original creators in 1966 of the first multidisciplinary pigmented lesion clinic for the management of patients with cutaneous melanoma. Trained in internal medicine, dermatology and pathology, he became one of the foremost dermatopathologists in the world. He is a consultant's consultant. His incomparable photographic memory enables him to recall cases he saw decades before. He is the consummate teacher who combines extraordinary knowledge with equally matching enthusiasm. He has been a teacher and mentor to hundreds of dermatology and pathology residents and at least two generations of dermatopathology fellows. He is still the "go to guy" for difficult pigmented lesions.

Biographical note prepared by Arthur J. Sober, MD

THE GRAND DAME OF FRUIT STREET

by Samuel O. Thier, MD

Dr. Holly Smith [Lloyd H. Smith, Jr., MD] returned to the MGH from his position as chief of Medicine at the University of California in San Francisco to speak at a reunion of MGH medical house staff in 1994 (one year after the MGH and Brigham and Women's Hospital merged to form Partners). Despite his lengthy absence he still called MGH home, and thought he had left the institution in responsible hands.

However, he allowed upon his return (obliquely commenting on the merger) that he was shocked to see the "Grande Dame of Fruit Street" (MGH) cavorting with the "Strumpet of Shattuck Street" (BWH).

SURGICAL TRAINING

by Andrew L. Warshaw, MD

**It was not until 1948 that the
chief resident in surgery was a Catholic (Bill McDermott);
1957 for a Jewish chief resident (Ed Salzman);
1978 for a woman (Sue Briggs);
1994 for an African-American
(Ed Barksdale and Lynt Johnson).**

When I got my internship in surgery at the MGH in 1963, the annual salary was $800 ($900 if you were married). By July, when I started, my salary was increased to $3,000, but they took away the Sunday dinner for families (which was not only the best meal of the week for everyone, but also a focal point for families to meet and make friendships) and, of course, taxes took away much of the pay raise.

Until 1971 surgical training was the same for every variety of "general" surgery. There were no fellowships for specialization in cardiac surgery, plastic surgery, transplantation, or anything else. Surgeons did a lot of learning on the job.

Sheila's Sign: Sheila was one of the special nurses who took care of Phillips House patients in the early days of cardiac surgery at the MGH, before a lot of technological aids. She knew when a patient needed to be returned to the OR by feeling the tube that drained blood from the chest after a heart operation: if it was warm, that meant rapid blood loss and the need to go back to stop the bleeding.

Claude Welch, MD, a surgical icon, was fast and efficient, both in the operating room and on rounds. He became known as "the grey ghost" because it was alleged that he could back out of a patient's room while entering it.

■ Andrew L. Warshaw, MD

A fine example of what is affectionately referred to as Preparation Triple H (i.e., graduate of Harvard College, Harvard Medical School, and a Harvard training program), Andy Warshaw joined the MGH surgical staff upon completion of his training and rapidly rose through the ranks to become full professor in 1987 and chair of the department in 1997. He is known worldwide for his contributions to the understanding of pancreatic disease and as a pioneer of modern pancreatic surgery. A clear and prolific writer, he has over 650 publications, including 35 in the *New England Journal of Medicine*. The impact of what he writes has been so great that, by one calculation, for the last 40 years every 18 hours somewhere in the world one of his papers is being cited.

Biographical note prepared by Carlos Fernandez-Del Castillo, MD

George S. Richardson, MD

When Partners was formed in 1993, uniting the MGH and Brigham and Women's Hospital, Dr. Richardson, who was still an active staff member, lamented

"This is truly the dawning of a new and unfamiliar age. I grew up with three enemies: Yale, the Soviet Union, and Brigham and Women's Hospital. Now there is only Yale."

I first met George Shattuck Richardson when I interviewed for a position at the MGH. In fact, it was George who had suggested I apply for the position. The day of the interview, before the hospital bigwigs, George welcomed me with a warm smile and outstretched hand and immediately made a panicky, anxious young man feel right at home. My other take on George that day was I was totally blown away by his energy. An elevator was available but he insisted we climb the three flights of stairs; he even raced me to the top. I could barely keep up with him. Fortunately I had just enough breath left to face the daunting MGH crew waiting on that third floor.

And so it was that I had the privilege of becoming a colleague of George at the legendary Vincent Hospital unit of the Mass General Hospital. From the start George was my advocate, my defender, my confidant, my friend. Day to day on the job I learned something special from him, and yet it was always George who'd thank *me* – as though it were I teaching him. As our offices abutted each other, I was able to observe with what respect and consideration and patience he treated each of his patients. The same sensitivity and respect extended to everyone in the hospital – the secretaries, the nurses, the physicians, and the hospital president. George was a masterful teacher. He was an incredible role model for the Harvard Medical students who came under his tutelage.

In another life, George traveled with presidents, senators, cabinet members, the occasional head of state, renowned physicians, brilliant scientists – you'd never guess it from his modest demeanor. His warmth, his humility, his eloquence, his admirable scientific achievements, his profound knowledge, his commitment to the causes of medicine and his equally broad appreciation of the arts charmed, won over everyone he met. That was George, the unassuming human being. Nor would you guess unless you were told that he came from one of the storied, distinguished families of Massachusetts. A genealogy that included presidents and other notables, his family, among other beneficent deeds, donated the land where Harvard Medical School is located, also the land for St. Paul's School, also a parcel of land along Cape Cod National Seashore. George was very proud of his brother Elliott, who stood up to a president at a time when the country was in peril. He was equally proud of his brother Peirson, an eminent researcher in the field of neuropathology. George had it all and he left an indelible legacy.

Biographical note prepared by Isaac Schiff, MD

■ Douglas J. Mathisen, MD

"When I came to MGH I envisioned an ivory tower environment – men in tweed jackets with leather elbow patches, smoking a pipe with a copy of the *New England Journal* sticking out of their back pocket. I have never seen anyone like that – just an institution and staff totally dedicated to patient care."

Doug Mathisen came to MGH for his surgical training after growing up and attending medical school in his native state of Illinois. After brief engagements at the NIH and Rush Medical School, his career followed an uninterrupted path at MGH. He eventually succeeded his friend and mentor Dr. Hermes Grillo as head of the storied Division of Thoracic Surgery. His many professional accomplishments include the presidency of the Society for Thoracic Surgery and the presidency of the Thoracic Surgery Program Directors Association and chair of its Residency Review Committee. His lifelong professional focus has been on patient care and especially resident training. He inherited from his school principal father a relentless commitment

to mind the details, which he relentlessly conveys to his residents on a daily and hourly basis. His determined nature comes gently wrapped in a genuine concern for his faculty and trainees as people, sprinkled with the homespun wisdom of a great storyteller.

Doug has four accomplished and talented daughters and is proud to have never missed one of their myriad sporting events in spite of his busy life and productivity. He and I have a special bond with similar roots, aspirations, and tastes – in homes, cars, music and sports – although he was apportioned far more hair when that was being handed out. Most significantly, we shared the good fortune of both having gotten remarried to MGH nurses in our own middle age and being granted the gift of their wonderful companionship as well as another chance at fatherhood.

Biographical note prepared by David F. Torchiana, MD

■ Peter L. Slavin, MD

"Our competition isn't Johns Hopkins and Mayo Clinic; it is cancer, heart disease and all the other diseases that cause suffering to mankind."

In referring to our thirst for innovation and to do all we can for our patients but also our need to be judicious, Dr. Peter Slavin, president of MGH, likes to say

"We have our feet on the gas pedal and the brake at the same time."

No one was prouder than Peter Slavin when in the year following the hospital's bicentennial the MGH was recognized in the leading survey of its kind as the number one hospital in the country. Peter had a special reason to be so proud. As a native of Malden, just a short way to the north, his family had for generations received care at MGH and the institution had a special stature in his mind as he grew up. His great grandfather, an Eastern European immigrant, received free care and dressing changes for chronic osteomyelitis at MGH for almost two decades. His photo hangs in Peter's conference room as a reminder of the hospital's roots and its mission.

Peter was a multi-sport athlete at the Buckingham Browne & Nichols School as were his two sons. He also recently served as the chair of its Board of Trustees. After BB&N, he attended Harvard as an undergraduate, where he met his wife Lori. Harvard Medical School, internal medicine residency at MGH and Harvard Business School then followed. He has been a lifer in the MGH administration since except for a brief deployment to St Louis. He became head of the Mass General Physicians Organization in 1999 and then president of the MGH in 2003.

Peter is an extraordinary fundraiser. He is dedicated to the clinical and scientific missions of the hospital and always goes the extra mile for the community mission to make sure we care just as well for the most vulnerable and unfortunate as we do for the privileged. His accomplishments have been great but he remains grounded with simple tastes and a love for sports. His success on the golf course may wax and wane but his passion for the game never does.

Biographical note prepared by David F. Torchiana, MD

■ David F. Torchiana, MD

"One of the attributes of doctors is that they are not only unmoved by lofty rhetoric but actually repelled by it."

I met David Torchiana early in my career at the MGH when I was working on an initiative to improve quality and efficiency at the hospital. Our data showed that Cardiac Surgery's length of stay was much longer than that of other teaching hospitals. The chief of Cardiac Surgery at the time was not interested in the data, so he referred me to a young surgeon on the staff. That surgeon was Torch.

I didn't know Torch well, but I certainly knew of him. I knew he was an incredibly talented cardiac surgeon with extraordinary clinical acumen and great teaching abilities. But what I didn't expect – but was soon to find out – was just how fascinated Torch was with data, with getting to the bottom of things, with drilling down deep to understand nuances. Through Torch's leadership and the multidisciplinary team he assembled, cardiac surgical care at MGH got much better and more efficient. Even more memorable for me was that this interaction kicked off a 20-year friendship and a great partnership that I've been so grateful to have.

When I became president of Mass General, and the position of CEO and chair of the Mass General Physicians Organization (MGPO) opened up, I was thrilled that Torch expressed an interest in the role. I couldn't imagine a better colleague. And Torch has never failed to deliver. He has been a spectacular and inspiring leader of the PO. He has found innovative ways to support the best physician staff on the planet, and he has worked hard to make their lives better. Humble and soft-spoken, Torch is a straight shooter whose presence at this hospital is powerful and reassuring.

A native of Illinois, Torch is the son of an Anglo-Irish literature professor at Northwestern University, and his family spent a number of years in Ireland. After graduating from Yale, Torch traveled to Churchill College at Cambridge, England, to work in the lab of Robert Geoffrey Edwards, who later won the Nobel Prize for his work in the field of in vitro fertilization. Torch then went to Harvard Medical School, followed by residency in surgery then cardiac surgery at MGH. Joining the MGH department of Surgery in 1989, he earned a reputation as a highly skilled, versatile and compassionate heart surgeon. He took over as chief of Cardiac Surgery in 1997, leading the division until 2003, when he assumed the reins of the MGPO.

On a personal note, I have learned over the years never to try to predict what Torch is going to say. Perhaps it is his strong literary roots that give him such a depth of insight, wisdom and a creative approach to problem solving. When you ask Torch a question, seek his opinion or go to him with a challenge, you can be sure that he will offer a thoughtful – usually unexpected – analysis and suggestion that is not just elegant but always right on the money.

Biographical note prepared by Peter L. Slavin, MD

■ Ernesto Gonzalez, MD

"There is no sacrifice when giving to those in need."

Dr. Ernesto Gonzalez is a professor of Dermatology at Harvard Medical School. He was lured to MGH in 1976 by Dr. Thomas Fitzpatrick to be the first director of the Phototherapy Unit. He became a pioneer in the treatment of psoriasis and other skin disorders.

Dr. Gonzalez was born in Puerto Rico, where he went to medical school before serving as a battalion surgeon for the U.S. Army in Vietnam, where he earned a Bronze Star. Upon arriving for fellowship training at Harvard Medical School, Dr. Gonzalez found himself to be one of very few Latinos in an elitist institution. He became a dogged advocate and inspiring leader who helped bring diversity to the medical school and to the hospital he cherishes so dearly. He served as the associate director of the Multicultural Affairs Office at MGH for over a decade and has received innumerable awards, including the prestigious Harold Amos Diversity Award from Harvard Medical School. In 2005, MGH established the Ernesto Gonzalez, MD, Award for Outstanding Community Service to honor him and to recognize MGH employees each year for their contributions to the Hispanic community.

Humble and self-effacing, Dr. Gonzalez quietly began monthly clinics in 1994 for homeless men and women at the medical respite facility of the Boston Health Care for the Homeless Program (BHCHP), where he trains a generation of dermatology residents to care for this vulnerable and excluded population. This clinic is now a formal clinical rotation for residents in the dermatology program.

Upon receiving an award for his service to BHCHP in 2011, Dr. Gonzalez honored the memory of his mother, who had grown up poor and homeless and had experienced discrimination for being black in Puerto Rico. Yet, he related, she had "elevated herself above human cruelty to demonstrate that she could be good and caring to others without bias." Dr. Gonzalez told the audience that her three siblings and his father all succumbed to tuberculosis when he and his brother were very young, yet she never lost her zest for life or her determination to give her children a better life.

Biographical note prepared by James J. O'Connell, III, MD

Susan M. Briggs, MD, MPH

"In a disaster, everyone is your neighbor, regardless of political, cultural or religious considerations. During the Bam, Iran earthquake, even the Iranian Army soldiers who were guarding us helped dig latrines in the sand for our USA team. Medicine is often the only victor in a disaster."

Editors' note: This is reminiscent of the quotation from distinguished Boston physicians John Collins Warren and James Jackson, the founders of the MGH, in their Circular Letter of 1810 seeking funds to build a new hospital:

"... It must always be considered the first duties to visit and to heal the sick. When in distress, every man becomes our neighbour."

Susan Briggs was born in Alexandra, Virginia. She first came to the MGH in 1965 as a staff nurse on the East Surgical Service. At that time she notably demonstrated keen intelligence and a consuming interest in surgical patients and their care. Eight years later, in 1974, and after graduating from the Loyola University, Stritch School of Medicine, she returned to the MGH as a resident in General Surgery, serving as the chief resident on the West Surgical Service in 1978-79. This was followed by two years as an NIH fellow in burn and trauma research at the University of California. Then, in 1985, and after three years as an assistant professor at the University of Louisville, she returned to the MGH. She rose to the rank of associate professor of Surgery at Harvard Medical School and visiting surgeon at the MGH. In 1998 she earned the degree of Master of Public Health from the Harvard School of Public Health.

Dr. Briggs is widely known for her compassion, her steadfast devotion to teaching and mentoring, her energy and enthusiasm, her persistence and calm under stress, and her many national and international contributions to the fields of trauma management and disaster relief. The work of her early years centered on the clinical practice of general and vascular surgery but she gradually focused on the practice of, and teaching and administrative activities related to, trauma management and disaster relief. She was instrumental in originating and administering a large number of national and international courses on trauma, burns and disaster response management. She served as the supervising medical officer for numerous deployments of medical teams by the National Disaster Medical System and the U.S. International Medical Surgical Response Team. These included assignment to actual and potential disaster sites in the continental United States, and to sites of major disasters in Haiti, Iran, China and Armenia. For this body of work she received special recognition from a number of organizations, including the National Disaster Medical System's Outstanding Achievement Award and the New England Surgical Society's Nathan Smith Distinguished Service Award. She was featured in the NIH National Library of Medicine exhibition "Changing the Face of Medicine: Celebrating America's Women Physicians."

Biographical note prepared by Leslie W. Ottinger, MD

The Baker Building

THE BAKER BRICK

by Lloyd Axelrod, MD, and Stephen P. Dretler, MD

The Baker Memorial Building, opened in 1931 and demolished in 1992 to make room for the Blake Building, was a 325-bed facility for patients of moderate means. Patients were charged a single fee for all services, adjusted on a sliding scale according to their ability to pay. This payment plan was revolutionary in its day and widely copied by other hospitals. During demolition intact individual bricks were piled outside the White 1 corridor on the Bulfinch patio. A member of the staff could not bear to see the destruction of the venerable building, collected the least damaged bricks, glued on each a brass plaque that read "MGH Baker Building 1931–1991" and distributed them to 40 colleagues. A senior medical staff person, upon receiving one of the bricks, held it to his ear and exclaimed:

"I can hear the footsteps of giants."

"We do the ordinary 'routine' very well. However, I believe strongly that the MGH has a higher calling – that our overriding mandate is to take on the extraordinary. In many instances, we represent for desperately ill patients their last best hope."

— *Roman W. DeSanctis, MD*

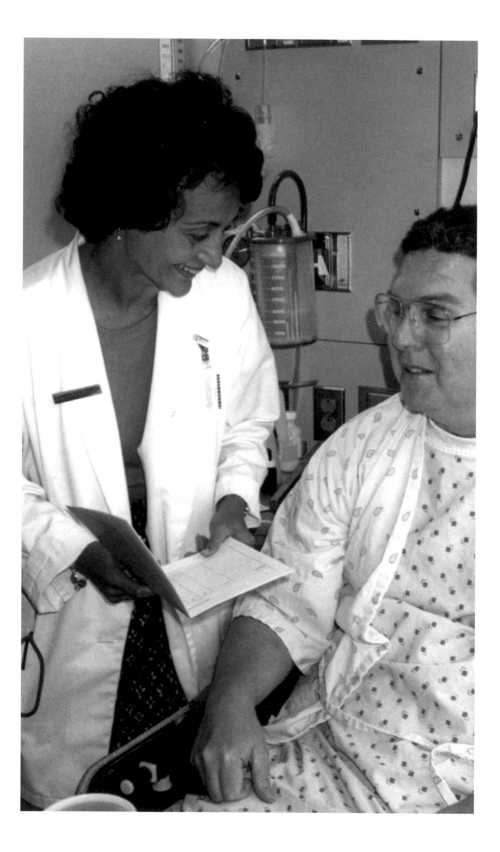

THE NURSES

Biographical notes for THE NURSES prepared by Georgia W. Peirce

Yvonne L. Munn, RN, MSN

"MGH nurses will do what they have always done through many transitions – hold to their ideals and initiate and support the changes that must be made."

**"Develop a spirit of inquiry.
If you begin to ask questions about your own practice,
on every aspect of it, and you don't like the answer
on some of those, then study it and change it.
That's what research is."**

Throughout her long and distinguished career, Yvonne L. Munn, associate general director and director of Nursing, promoted patient-focused, evidence-driven and research-based practice. Her commitment to collaborative practice and skill as a consensus builder enabled Munn to influence the practice of nursing and patient care services in the institutions with which she was affiliated. Her legacy of leadership during her tenure at the MGH from 1984 to 1993 positioned the department of Nursing to achieve the success it enjoys today.

The Yvonne L. Munn Center for Nursing Research was established in 2008 to build upon existing research initiatives including the annual lecture and awards program, doctoral nurse forum, the Norman Knight Visiting Professor program, and post-doctoral fellowships. The Munn Center serves as the platform for building a nursing research program that is clinically focused and advances the work of nurses. By providing opportunities to challenge current thinking and identifying new ways to shape and influence professional standards, patient care is enhanced, and opportunities to promote health through clinical inquiry are advanced.

Munn, a native of Edmonton, Canada, had a nursing career that spanned more than 40 years. Her first nursing leadership position was as a science instructor at Edmonton General School of Nursing. Two years later she assumed the position of assistant director of Nursing at Alberta's Medicine Hat General Hospital and education director for that hospital's school of nursing. In 1956, she moved to the United States when she accepted a position as assistant director of Nursing Services at Sharp Memorial Hospital in San Diego, California.

Munn continued her leadership journey at Presbyterian-St. Luke's Hospital in Chicago, Ill. She began as the division of Nursing's assistant chairperson for education and research in 1969. By the time she left, eight years later, she held the positions of assistant vice president for Nursing at Rush Presbyterian-St. Luke's Medical Center and associate dean of Rush College of Nursing. Prior to coming to the MGH, she was vice president for Nursing Services, vice president for Patient Services and vice president for Patient Systems and Evaluation at Methodist Hospitals of Dallas, Texas.

Jeanette Ives Erickson, RN, DNP

"If you keep your eye on the patient, you will always be headed in the right direction."

Dr. Ives Erickson, senior vice president for Patient Care and chief nurse, is responsible for clinical practice, research, education and community

service, serving 5,300 nurses, health professionals and support staff. In addition, she serves as the chair of the Chief Nurse Council for Partners HealthCare. She is an instructor at Harvard Medical School and an assistant professor at the MGH Institute of Health Professions. She is a fellow in the American Academy of Nursing and a past Robert Wood Johnson executive nurse fellow, where her research focused on the role of the chief nurse within integrated health care systems. In 2007, she was appointed by the Secretary of Health and Human Services to serve on the U.S. National Advisory Council on Nurse Education and Practice.

Dr. Ives Erickson has developed new measures to evaluate innovations that influence professional nursing practice, including The Professional Practice Environment Scale that is used to evaluate nurses' and other clinicians' perceptions and satisfaction with the professional practice environment in which they work. This psychometrically accurate instrument is being used by more than 100 health care institutions in fifteen countries, and has been translated into multiple languages including Chinese, Finnish, Turkish and Spanish.

She has presented and consulted throughout the world on a variety of issues affecting nurse autonomy, leadership development, collaborative decision-making, and Magnet Hospital designation.

Thelma J. Wells, RN, PhD

"It's almost as if all generations of graduates are with us on this night ... the ghosts of classes past."

— Thelma Wells, RN, PhD, class of 1962, speaking at the final MGH School of Nursing Graduation Ceremony in June 1981

That year, the MGH made the difficult decision to close its School of Nursing. This was an event years in the making. As the school celebrated its centennial in 1973, its future seemed uncertain, as nursing education was rapidly shifting to a collegiate model. Ruth Sleeper, RN, class of 1922, former director of the School of Nursing and department of Nursing, urged John Knowles, MD, the hospital's general director, to have the

MGH petition the Massachusetts Board of Higher Education to confer degree-granting authority to the MGH Educational Division.

In 1977, the Board granted MGH's request, paving the way for postgraduate certificate and master's-degree-level programs to be offered by the MGH. Natalie Petzold, RN, the director of the School of Nursing, co-chaired a committee to explore degree-granting status and the feasibility of establishing a freestanding interdisciplinary graduate school. In 1980, the hospital formally established the interdisciplinary MGH Institute of Health Professions, and a year later the celebrated Massachusetts General Hospital School of Nursing graduated its last class and closed its doors.

A new MGH era in nursing education began in 1982, when the Institute's Graduate Program in Nursing admitted its first entry-level master's students. This was the country's first hospital-based graduate degree program and one of the first to enroll baccalaureate-prepared individuals with no prior experience or education in nursing.

■ Patricia Beckles, RN

"If they could breathe for a few minutes on their own you could take them out of the respirator for short periods. I can remember the look of joy on their faces while they were out, and the look of anxiety when they had to return to the respirator."

Patricia Beckles, RN, was a night nurse in MGH Pediatrics for 50 years and continued to work per diem for many years thereafter. According to hospital records, she has amassed the longest record of service of any MGH nurse in the history of the hospital. During her five-decade-plus career, she witnessed phenomenal change at MGH and within health care, including the evolution of newborn care and efforts to diversify the hospital and its nursing staff.

In 1955, before the Salk vaccine became available, an epidemic of poliomyelitis occurred in the Boston area, taxing the facilities of the MGH and its Nursing Service. The ninth floor of the White Building was quickly emptied to set up a respirator unit, and "Polio Teams" were organized to provide round-the-clock care. In total, 428 patients were admitted with polio in some form – 376 adults and 52 children. Of those, 73 adults and eight children were in respirators for varying periods of time. As of January 1956, there were still 30 patients in respirators.

■ Karen Lipshires, RN-BC, MS-HMP

Heard and repeated over the years (source unknown):

"Physicians figure out 'what's wrong,' nurses figure out the 'so what.'"

Karen Lipshires, chemotherapy order set coordinator, MGH Cancer Center, recently marked her 35th anniversary working as a nurse at MGH. She has worked for a variety of services throughout her career, including Neurosciences, Orthopedics and Medicine. Today she is part of a team that creates templates for chemotherapy ordering, including dosing and side effect management. The team contributes to helping patients better tolerate their treatment and to ensuring the smooth, safe and consistent delivery of care. "Physicians figure out 'what's wrong,' nurses figure out the 'so what'" has become her dinner table response to the commonly asked question: What's the difference between what doctors and nurses do?

■ Ruth Sleeper, RN, MS

"Always, always more to see, more to learn, more to do ... to improve both care and cure."

Ruth Sleeper is widely credited with raising the professional standards for nursing nationwide. Sleeper graduated from the MGH School of Nursing in 1922 and became a staff nurse at the hospital. From 1933 to 1946, she served as the assistant superintendent of Nursing and assistant principal of the School of Nursing. From 1947 to 1966, she served as the director of both the MGH School of Nursing and the hospital's Nursing Service – a time when nursing was evolving from a hospital-based apprenticeship into a profession requiring academic training and practical experience. Her decision to revise the school's curriculum to reflect this shift was considered revolutionary, yet soon became the standard for nurses' training. She was a firm supporter of academic education and worked to establish affiliations with colleges and universities to ensure that nurses would have a broader academic base and a degree. Even after her retirement she continued to work to transform the MGH School of Nursing into a degree-granting school.

Nationally, Sleeper served as president of the National League of Nursing Education and later as the first president of the National League for Nursing. She was chair of the Nursing Advisory Committee of the Veteran's Administration; member of the National Nursing Council for War Service; member of the Health Resources Advisory Committee, Office of Defense Mobilization, U.S. State Department; consultant to the U.S. Public Health Service Division of Nursing Education; and member of the American Red Cross Advisory Board on Health and Human Services, among others.

Sleeper was also well known and respected internationally. She served as chair of the Education Committee of the International Council of Nursing (1947–1961), as a member of the Expert Committee on Nursing of the World Health Organization, with the Florence Nightingale International Foundation, and as a member of the Commission on the Status of Women at a meeting of the Economic and Social Council of the United Nations.

President Dwight D. Eisenhower presents his pen to Ruth Sleeper
after he declared National Nurse Week in 1954.

■ Susan L. Fisher, RN

**"As new nursing students, we were taught never, never
to refer to the hospital as 'Mass General.'
Our options were to use the full name or 'MGH.'
'The General' was accepted only grudgingly."**

Susan L. Fisher graduated from the MGH School of Nursing in 1966 and
began working as an MGH staff nurse on Bulfinch 3, then the Medical
ICU. Her entire career was then spent at the MGH. From 1972 to 1984,
she served as the Boston Visiting Nurse Association (VNA) liaison to the
hospital, working full-time at MGH while employed by the VNA. Then from
1984 until her retirement in 2006 she worked in the MGH Social Service
Department Coordinated Care Program. In her "retirement," she continues to
be an active volunteer with the MGH Nurses' Alumnae Association, serving
as editor of *The Alumnae Record* and as co-historian. She has participated in
numerous alumnae-supported projects, including collecting members' oral
histories, cataloguing and preserving the MGH School of Nursing archives,
and contributing to the publication of *MGH Nursing at Two Hundred* to
commemorate the hospital's bicentennial. Fisher also is an active volunteer
with both the MGH Archives and Special Collections Program and the
Ladies Visiting Committee.

■ Sylvia Perkins, RN, BS, MA

"Probably the chief bonus of the plan in nursing service situations was not so much the administrative advantages as it was the increased recognition of the value of every member of the team."

Sylvia Perkins, class of 1928, served as assistant director of the MGH School of Nursing from 1941 to 1966. She was also the author of *A Centennial Review: The Massachusetts General Hospital School of Nursing,* in which she observed that the end of World War II did not mean an increase in registered nurses at the hospital. Instead, there was an increase of auxiliary staff – nursing orderlies, licensed practical nurses and hospital aides. In order to make effective use of this staffing shift, provide maximum care for the patients, improve the effectiveness of the head nurse, and promote harmonious relationships and job satisfaction for all staff, the Team Plan seemed to hold the answer. The basic concept centered on having every member of a care team think in terms of "our" patient versus "my" patient.

■ Jean Ridgway Tienken, RN

"The hospital had been 'disaster planning' in the event that the war reached American soil, so when the Cocoanut Grove fire occurred, we were ready to handle multiple casualties. That preparation alone may have saved who knows how many lives."

Jean Ridgway Tienken, class of 1945, worked on the wards as a student nurse the night of the Cocoanut Grove fire. On November 28, 1942, nearly one thousand people crowded into the Cocoanut Grove nightclub to party. Within an hour, a raging fire left 492 dead and hundreds injured and in Boston hospitals. MGH received 114 casualties: 39 living and 75 who were either dead on arrival or shortly after admission. The Cocoanut Grove fire demonstrated what being prepared really could mean in terms of saving lives. The hospital's response to those injured in the fire helped to create more effective resources for dealing with major emergencies in Boston. Fittingly, the hospital referred to its disaster plan internally as "Operation Cocoanut" for many years.

■ Ruth Dempsey, RN

"Ms. Macdonald made the change that was perhaps waiting to happen. Not merely a pass-through but a change, a good call to action, to care, to think, to improvise, to triage, to do what was right for the patient at that moment, not what had been tradition. She felt that change was not to be feared. Orientations and education were where nurses could learn and be mentored and that included leadership mentoring for head nurses. So that by the end of her tenure as the hospital moved to specialized units, the head nurse had a true leadership position. And staff on the units became experts to give the best possible care to the patient."

Ruth Dempsey, retired nurse manager of the Thoracic Surgical Unit, graduated in 1964 from the University of Maine in Orono just one mile from her family home. She and a classmate immediately headed to Boston to "try it out for a year." She became a staff nurse on the Baker 3 Urology Unit at a time when specialty units were rare. Still seeking adventure, she traveled to Europe before returning to MGH as a float nurse. After a year she became the assistant head nurse, and a year later head nurse of the Baker 10 General Surgery Unit, a position she held for five years. In 1970, Dr. Hermes Grillo recruited Dempsey as head nurse of the new Thoracic Surgical Unit he was starting. She remained at the helm  there for three decades that saw many changes in both nursing and surgical procedures. With an eye toward retirement, Dempsey transitioned into a staff specialist role and later became an advocate for unit service associates, ably integrating them into the fabric of the MGH. Today, "retirement" finds her working one day a week in The Maxwell & Eleanor Blum Patient and Family Learning Center.

Ruth Farrisey, RN

"Around 1960, Dr. John Stoeckle asked if a
nurse clinic could be run in his medical clinic on Friday
afternoons. It expanded to Wednesday and Friday afternoons
and reinforced the role of nurses as the pivotal persons for
the patient and the family.

"Then in late 1964, Dr. Jack Connolly, a pediatrician,
asked for a meeting to discuss the development of the
pediatric nurse practitioner program after a model of the one
he visited in Colorado. It started with a pediatric practitioner
in 1968, as the pediatric physicians were the first to want the
nurse in an expanded role.

"In 1970, the adult nurse practitioner program started.
[We] had to separate pediatric from adult as the emphasis for
the adult was on chronic disease follow up, and in pediatrics it
was on wellness and maintenance of wellness before looking
at illness. By the mid-'70s, the Primary Care Physician
Program combined with the Adult Nurse Practitioner
Program. Protocols were written by the nurses to reinforce
the role of the nurse practitioner. The doctors clearly were
interested and supportive so there was never a protocol
rejected by the Executive Committee."

Ruth Farrisey, MGH School of Nursing, class of 1938, had a distinguished career as a clinician; senior administrator at MGH and its Neighborhood Health Centers including service as associate director, department of Nursing for Ambulatory Care; advocate for health care access for all; and faculty member of the MGH School of Nursing and later the MGH Institute. According to John Stoeckle, MD, Farrisey, director of Nursing and assistant director of clinics, was a key contributor to the introduction of the hospital's off-site outpatient clinics. She was "always around, always looking to make things better. Operationally she really ran the clinic, because the nurses ran admissions." She was known as a visionary advocate for the advanced practice nursing role and a strong leader in the development of collaborative nursing and medical practice. As described, in 1968 MGH introduced a pediatric nurse practitioner program, only the second in the country.

■ Marlene Norton, RN

"When primary nursing came into being in the 1970s, it reflected all the thoughts and ideas I had from this period. I came into pediatrics to care not just for the child but the family. As a nurse it is rewarding when you see the child recover, saddening when a child is lost and enlightening because you always learn from the experience."

Marlene Norton was a 1961 graduate of the MGH School of Nursing. By the 1970s, primary nursing was the practice model for the MGH Pediatric Service. As a patient and family arrived on the unit, a nurse would take responsibility for the family as a primary nurse with others as secondary nurses. This allowed the family and the child to bond with "their nurse," who could give the best possible care and be available for the child and family during the admission and any future admissions to the unit. In other areas of nursing the concept was just starting to be considered.

■ Ada Plumer, RN

"In the late '60s and early '70s, Ada Plumer recognized the need for IV therapy information beyond MGH. Teams were starting to form and were floundering for information. She and Marge Knight, supervisor of IV Therapy at Johns Hopkins, had communicated and decided to start a national organization so that quality standards for the practice could be established."

— submitted by Susan Pauley, RN, nurse manager, MGH IV Team

Intravenous (IV) therapy provides an enduring example of a rapidly growing MGH service provided by nurses that also left its mark nationally and internationally. The service started in 1940 at the MGH with one nurse, Ada Plumer, RN, MGH School of Nursing, class of 1938. In her first year, she answered 300 calls for IV therapy. By 1961, the service had grown to a staff of nine nurses who carried out some 42,000 procedures for patients in the Phillips House and the Baker Memorial Building. Believed to be the first person ever to hold the title "IV nurse," in 1973 Plumer cofounded the National Intravenous Therapy Association, now the Infusion Nurses Society.

■ Barbara Teixeira Goral, RN

"I was privileged to be a mentor, supervisor and educator to the new nurses in the unit. Their transition to competent respiratory ICU nurses was facilitated at a rate much faster than before and with much less stress."

In the late 1960s, under the leadership of Mary Macdonald, chief of the MGH Nursing Service from 1968 to 1983, MGH broadened the scope of nurses by introducing the unit teacher role. Barbara Teixeira Goral, MGH School of Nursing, class of 1967, was the first unit teacher in the Respiratory ICU. The concept was later duplicated throughout the country. The goal was to have unit teachers available on the patient care units. The basic premise was that nurses had to change, think, process, advocate and constantly learn. A centralized staff education department could not foster this development for each individual. The unit teacher was responsible to the clinical leader on the unit, who supervised new graduates. This had a positive impact on staff retention, which had become a major issue.

Barbara Teixeira Goral at the dedication of the Vietnam Women's Memorial, located on the National Mall in Washington, DC. Approximately 10,000 women — mostly nurses, including Goral — served in Vietnam. Photo courtesy of the Boston Herald

Roberta Keene Nemeskal, RN

"As the Vietnam War escalated, the U.S. Army enhanced nursing recruitment efforts through its U.S. Army Student Nurse Program. Nursing students entering their last one or two years of nursing school were recruited as inactive enlisted personnel receiving private grade [E-2] monthly pay. Following their nursing school graduation, participants were commissioned as officers in the Army Nurse Corps and served on active duty for two to three years."

The 1960s marked a time when the United States became very involved in the war in Vietnam. In the wake of World War II the United States had passed the National Defense Act of 1947, in which nursing was declared an essential service. Given the subsequent expansion of the military nursing service and increased nursing participation in the civil defense program, MGH hosted a pilot program specifically to train nurses for Vietnam. Roberta Keene Nemeskal, MGH School of Nursing, class of 1969, was among the trainees.

Roberta Nemeskal during her training for Vietnam

■ Mary Macdonald, RN, MA

"I told Dr. Knowles [MGH general director] that I would only take the job if it was as chief of the Nursing Service so that nursing would be on the same level as the other services that had chiefs. One of my first acts as chief was to change the name to the Department of Nursing, to better reflect the patient care, teaching and research aspects of the profession."

"Our objective will be to ... create an environment in which the nurse can function as a participating member of the total health team."

Mary Macdonald was an author, researcher, activist and nursing leader who earned a reputation as a visionary throughout her four-decade career. A 1942 graduate of the MGH School of Nursing, Macdonald began her career in academia, and later returned to the MGH as director of Analytic Studies in Nursing. In 1968 she became chief of the Nursing Service, a position she held until 1983. It was a time of social and value-laden revolutions in the United States, with the start of the Vietnam War and the civil rights movement. Within the hospital, the number of intensive care units was increasing dramatically, having a profound impact on the recruitment and responsibilities of nurses.

Macdonald described the profession of nursing at that time as being in a "becoming stage," and her goal was to establish a system of delivering care that would permit the nurse to nurse in the true sense of the professional mission. Macdonald was also responsible for broadening the scope of nurses by introducing the unit teacher role, a move that was replicated in hospitals across the country. By her own assessment, though,

"My greatest accomplishment was the freedom I gave to staff with the idea that no matter where you were in the line you had something to offer."

"It's the nurse who is the single, most essential factor"

in the future success of telediagnosis.

— *Kenneth T. Bird, MD, an early pioneer in the field*

Prompted by a devastating plane crash in Boston in 1961, two years later the MGH became the first general hospital in the United States to establish and operate a medical station at an international airport. The Logan Airport Medical Station offered health services to residents of East Boston, airport employees and several million travelers annually.

Five full-time nurses provided 24-hour coverage, and in 1968 they established direct communication with the MGH through a telecommunication system that made advice and necessary physician orders immediately available. The medical station was connected by two-way television with the MGH Emergency Ward. Patients were triaged and treated by a staff of nurse practitioners, with medical consultation available through a television circuit. This is believed to have been the first use of telemedicine for general patient care and physical diagnosis.

■ Keith W. Perleberg, RN, MDiv

"It's all about providing Excellence Every Day."

Keith Perleberg served the MGH community for two decades and left an indelible mark. He started at the hospital in 1991 as a staff nurse on the Psychiatry Unit, where he was later appointed interim nurse manager. In 2001 he was named nursing director for Phillips House 20 and 21. He became known as an advocate for patient and staff safety, serving in leadership roles on several committees, including the Magnet Redesignation Committee. His talent and passion for providing the highest quality, patient- and family-centered care led to his appointment in 2007 as the first director of the Patient Care Services Office of Quality & Safety. Throughout his five years in this role, he worked tirelessly to ingrain quality and safety into the hospital culture. Just prior to his sudden and unexpected death in 2012, he was named a recipient of the prestigious Partners HealthCare Nesson Award, honoring innovation in medical practice and interdisciplinary collaboration. A granite memorial bench on the Bulfinch lawn that was dedicated to his memory is inscribed: "In loving memory of Keith W. Perleberg, RN, MDiv: A dear friend, cherished colleague and true champion of excellence in every way."

■ Diane Smith, RN

"At our second-year capping ceremony,
Dr. Ellsworth Neumann, vice president of the MGH,
said 'Ladies – as we were always called in the era –
remember to always touch your patient
no matter how much of a hurry you may be in.
Even if you just touch their foot on the way out
of the room, touch your patients.'"

"We always had 7am Friday morning meetings
for the outpatient nurses. Miss Ruth Farrisey would say:
'Ladies, ladies, I have provided you many articles so
that you are always informed about the bigger world of
medicine and nursing. You must be informed.'
We would walk away with
four or five articles each week."

"I clearly remember Dr. John Stoeckle saying:
'If you do not know where the patient was
born and raised, if you do not know what
type of work they do, and if you do not
know about their family, you have not
done a complete physical.'"

Diane Smith graduated from the MGH School of Nursing in 1966 and then earned her BA in sociology from Emmanuel College. In the early 1970's Smith was one of the nursing pioneers who became a nurse practitioner in MGH's certificate program, one of only two such programs in the United States at the time. Dedicated to lifelong learning, she most recently participated in the Nursing Ethics Residency at MGH. She has been a member of the hospital's nursing staff off-and-on for many years, with out-of-state detours that each led back to MGH, evidence of her often-heard assertion that

"There is no place quite like MGH."

Smith has been at the hospital continuously since 1999, first in outpatient internal medicine and most recently in the MGH Cancer Center, currently working as an access nurse in the Termeer Center for Targeted Therapies. Smith was an MGH Nurses' Alumnae Association board member from 1998 to 2005, serving as president for the final two years. During her tenure on the board, she was active in raising the necessary funds to commission the nursing sundial sculpture now located on the Bulfinch lawn.

■ Dorothy A. Jones, RN, EdD

"The essence of professional nursing is centered within the relationship between the patient (family and community) and the nurse. This focus on relationship has been nursing's history and is the hallmark of our existence. Patients require precisely that which nursing, by heritage and current practice, is uniquely qualified to offer."

In 2007, Dorothy A. Jones became the first director of The Yvonne L. Munn Center for Nursing Research. She currently divides her time between this role at MGH and Boston College, where she is professor of Adult Health Nursing in the William F. Connell School of Nursing. She is also a visiting professor at the University of Navarra and the Clinica de Navarra in Pamplona, Spain. As director of the Munn Center, she has the opportunity to advance a research agenda across the MGH community and to promote opportunities for nurse researchers to develop their own programs of research. Between the two roles, she has developed several areas of research concentration including development and evaluation of nursing theory, language development and classification, instrument development, workforce evaluation and intervention research, especially around coaching and recovery at home after surgery.

Dr. Jones began working as a nurse scientist in the MGH Department of Quality Assurance, Research and Staff Development in 1988. In 2000 she became a senior nurse scientist, continuing her cultivation of nursing research and scholarship throughout the MGH Department of Nursing. In her initial years at the helm of the Munn Center, she identified the infrastructure and resources required to support nursing research at MGH, promoted a culture of inquiry, and promoted the implementation and evaluation of a variety of innovative initiatives, including the Munn Post Doctoral Fellowship, the Nurse Scientist Advancement Model, the Clinical Nurse Specialist Research Task Force and the Connell Nursing Research Scholars group.

Widely regarded as a prominent figure within the nursing research world, Dr. Jones has more than 130 publications in leading journals and has authored or co-authored 14 books.

She presents internationally and consults on multiple issues affecting nursing education, clinical practice and research. She is the recipient of numerous teaching and mentoring awards. She has been the recipient of grant funding from the National Institute of Nursing Research of the NIH, the division of Nursing, specialty organizations, and foundations. Her scholarship continues to support the advancement of nursing knowledge and professional practice to improve care for patients and their families.

■ Brian French, RN, MS

"'You work until your life is done, and you live until your work is done' is the valuable lesson that helped shape my understanding of the value and meaning of my work as a clinician, educator and director at MGH."

Brian French, director of the Maxwell & Eleanor Blum Patient and Family Learning Center, has been a nurse at MGH since 1985.

"Working at MGH, we are privileged to learn so much of value from our experiences with patients and their families. One important lesson for me

came early in my career when I was a new staff nurse in the surgical ICU and caring for a 19-year old man. He was days away from heading to college and out on the town celebrating with friends when they noticed a group of men harassing a homeless person. As my patient stepped in to help, one of the attackers pushed him away, landing him in the path of a moving car. He was immediately struck, dragged a short distance and left with multiple, serious injuries.

"For the next month, I cared for him as he struggled to survive and for his family and friends as they tried to find meaning in all that had happened. They – and I – found some comfort in knowing this young man had been injured while trying to help a vulnerable person in need. Despite all that was done for him, my young patient's injuries proved too much for him to survive. It was when I was struggling to come to terms with this senseless tragedy that I first heard the phrase that has guided me throughout my career: 'You work until your life is done and you live until your work is done.' No matter how brief the time we may have, we all have the capacity to make a difference in the lives of others."

■ Lori Pugsley, RN, MEd

"Whatever is in the best interest of the patient is always the right answer to your question."

— said almost daily by Lori Pugsley when staff ask about placement, care or clinical decisions

Lori Pugsley is the nurse director for the Newborn Family Units at the MGH, with responsibility for two inpatient OB newborn family units and the care of infants in the postpartum, level 1 and level 2 newborn nurseries. Lori began her career as a staff nurse at MGH and today has more than 20 years of experience as a maternal-child nurse, with expertise in patient and staff education. Among her many accomplishments, she coordinated the hospital's Childbirth Education Program, overseeing a staff of 21 educators, and developed and implemented numerous programs for patients and staff. Pugsley has presented programs to nursing students, the general public and international audiences as a guest speaker. She is committed to advancing practice for perinatal, neonatal and women's health nurses, advocating for nurses and striving to improve care for all women.

Photo by Joshua Touster

■ Sally Millar, RN, MBA

"When you learn, teach; when you get, give."

Throughout her 45-year nursing career, Sally Millar distinguished herself as a pioneer in health informatics, developing systems to quantify patients' needs for nursing care and using data to establish appropriate levels of care. She also consistently served as a strong advocate for integrating respect for patient privacy into health information systems and patient safety initiatives.

She began her career at MGH as a cardiac surgery ICU staff nurse. Throughout her career she served in a variety of leadership positions including as director of the MGH Office of Patient Advocacy and The Maxwell & Eleanor Blum Patient and Family Learning Center and as co-chair of the MGH Clinical Policy and Records Committee and the Partners Confidentiality Program.

Her visionary work with acuity and staffing data helped identify trends, model lengths-of-stay, influence budgeting and staffing levels, conduct research, accurately forecast the needs of new patient care units coming online and improve other essential business functions of the hospital.

In addition, she was editor of *Methods in Critical Care – The American Association of Critical-Care Nurses (AACN) Manual,* the world's first manual of clinical procedures for critical care nurses. She continued as senior editor for the book's second edition, retitled *AACN Procedure Manual for Critical Care.* Now in its 6th edition, it has been adopted as the gold standard by nearly every critical care unit in the United States and many units in other countries.

A graduate of a hospital-based diploma nursing school, as an AACN national board member and its 1981 president Millar passionately advocated for nurses to obtain baccalaureate degrees and helped establish AACN's scholarship program, a signature initiative that is now supported by an endowment that exceeds $2 million. Millar later became one of the first nurses to earn a Master's of Business Administration degree.

Stevenson Morency, RN

"The experience I got at MGH broadened my horizons. I had great mentors ... and I am forever grateful to them for making themselves available to me when I needed their support."

Stevenson Morency joined the MGH community as a junior at the University of Massachusetts, Amherst, while working toward a Bachelor of Science in Nursing degree. Originally from Haiti, he was the first recipient of the Hausman Student Nurse Fellowship, awarded by the MGH Patient Care Services' Diversity Program in an effort to expand the diversity of the MGH nursing staff to reflect better the patient population and the population of the community as a whole. Morency spent his 10-week fellowship rotating between several MGH units, observing various roles and contributing as needed. He was a standout, and upon graduation Morency formally joined the MGH community as a staff nurse on the Churchill White 7 Surgical Unit, where he has worked for more than five years.

Barbara A. Dunderdale, RN

"This is MGH – Man's Greatest Hospital."

"Always a patient's room has a tendency to become a collect-all for more supplies than one can imagine. Many an instructor would suggest that for everything you brought into the room, leave with something else."

Upon graduating from the MGH School of Nursing in 1963, Barbara A. Dunderdale, nurse manager, Phillips House 20 and 22, White 7, 1970-2002, was hired as a staff nurse and soon after appointed head nurse on the

Orthopedic Service on White 5. Over the years she worked in both the White Building and Phillips House, assuming roles as nursing supervisor, nurse manager, and later nursing director, at one time for three individual patient care units. During the course of her 47-year nursing career, Dunderdale earned a reputation as a skilled, compassionate caregiver with quick humor, caring for countless patients. She was also an invaluable colleague, mentor and friend to her fellow nurses. Dunderdale has been an active member of the MGH Nurses' Alumnae Association and served as the group's president from 2008–2010. Although she formally "retired" in 2002, Dunderdale continues to serve the hospital's mission in the MGH Development Office, working with generous patients and families by advocating for their philanthropic interests to support programs, research, services and capital needs that serve the hospital's patients.

■ Edward Coakley, RN, MEd, MA, MSN

"You can't think outside the box if you're in it."

Ed Coakley had an extraordinary career at MGH as a nurse educator, interim chief nursing officer, operating room leader and founder of the nursing newsletter *Caring Headlines*. Throughout his 40-year career at MGH – from staff nurse to director emeritus of Nursing – Coakley was universally regarded as a free thinker of the highest order. He advanced the profession of nursing, prepared future providers, and ensured delivery of the best possible patient- and family-centered care. Coakley sparked a formal effort to preserve MGH nursing history through his photo essay "Tracing the Emergence of Professional Nursing at MGH: 1821–1960."

As director emeritus, he turned his attention to becoming an innovation specialist in The Center for Innovations in Care Delivery, a center within MGH Nursing and Patient Care Services. Coakley was among the first to examine the potential impact of an aging population on the delivery of care. In 2007, the Health Resources and Services Administration of the U.S. Department of Health and Human Services awarded him a $650,000 grant to support an innovative RN Residency Program: Transitioning to Geriatrics and Palliative Care. This initiative continues to help prepare the next generation of nurses to care for an aging population. It has the added benefit of helping to redesign the hospital workplace better to accommodate older nurses, leveraging their experience and knowledge to support newer nurses. This work came at a critical time, as a worldwide nursing shortage was worsening and older nurses were leaving the profession in large numbers. The approach was disseminated nationally under the program name ageWISE.

Coakley also advised nursing staff in the hospital's Medical ICU as it became one of four sites nationwide to be awarded funding from the Robert Wood Johnson Foundation to develop innovative demonstration projects. The "Merging Palliative Care and Critical Care Cultures Quality Demonstration Project" communicated its findings with national workgroups to address particular challenges to existing models of care. Examples include an open visiting policy, the role of the Palliative Care Service, Ethics Rounds and the work of palliative care nurse champions.

Carol A. Ghiloni, RN, MSN

"I've often heard it said – as a matter of teaching or polite persuasion – there's the right way, the wrong way and the MGH way."

Oncology nurse Carol A. Ghiloni, clinical educator in The Norman Knight Nursing Center for Clinical & Professional Development, has provided care to MGH patients for more than 45 years. One of the pioneers in oncology at MGH, Carol was founding nurse director of the Inpatient Oncology Unit, a position she held for four decades until her retirement.

Ghiloni started working at MGH in general medicine in the 60s and soon became an assistant head nurse and then nurse director. A leader in developing oncology nursing as a specialty here at the hospital, she advocated for a dedicated inpatient unit where nurses could gain expertise in the care of oncology patients. Now serving part-time as a clinical educator, Ghiloni is teaching nurses about chemotherapy administration as well as the hospital's new electronic medication system. The Cancer Center student nurse oncology fellowship program is named for Ghiloni in recognition of her great contribution to oncology nursing.

■ Joanne Parhiala, RN

"As I escorted the Magnet appraisers throughout MGH,
I couldn't have been more impressed or more proud."

Joanne Parhiala is an MGH staff nurse and was a Magnet ambassador, a liaison with the Magnet champions. In 2003, the MGH became the state's first hospital to earn Magnet Recognition from the American Nurses Credentialing Center, a subsidiary of the American Nurses Association. The credential is the highest honor an organization can receive for professional nursing practice. In 2008 and again in 2013, the hospital was redesignated a Magnet organization. To date, fewer than seven percent of all U.S. hospitals have received this recognition. Research demonstrates that Magnet hospitals have better patient outcomes, patient satisfaction and nursing satisfaction, as well as lower clinical nurse turnover.

"Nursing represents the heart and soul of this hospital."

— Peter L. Slavin, MD, president,
Massachusetts General Hospital